The Facilitators

Doris Manly
Loretto Browne
Valerie Cox
Nick Lowry

BRANDSMA BOOKS LIMITED

The Constitution of the New Ireland would provide for changes in the 1937 Irish Constitution necessary to ensure the creation of a national health service on the British model; a revised social security system; the removal of censorship; the right to legislate on such matters as family planning, abortion, and other personal liberties on the British model.

—The Right Hon. Harold Wilson, British Prime Minister, 1971.

ISBN 0 9511516 0 6 (hardback)
    0 9511516 1 4 (paperback)

Contents

by DORIS MANLY

CHAPTER 1

Who and Why

You are being "facilitated" every day. So am I. So are our children. The Facilitators are all around us all the time – working hard. Their self-appointed task is to change us: to alter our ways of looking at and feeling about reality, so that we will then behave as they want us to behave.

These Facilitators are working, not merely for "social change", but for certain highly-specific social changes. They "facilitate" change by trying to alter the attitudes and values of the public. Now that is fair enough; anyone working for any change, good or bad, must do that. But the Facilitators use methods which are manipulative, and therefore unfit for use on human beings: that is, on creatures upon whom God has bestowed dignity and freedom.

The human person acts freely when he deliberately chooses to behave in a manner consistent with what he cognises about reality – including moral reality. That is, when his behaviour is dictated by what he judges to be objectively true and good.

In order to make such judgements in any situation a person needs three things. He needs to know the facts of the case. He needs to have some objective norms in mind by which to judge. And he needs the habit of reason: he needs to be well used to applying those objective standards to actual cases, in order to work out what course of action is best. He needs to be able to *think*.

The Facilitators do not want the "facilitated" – that is, you and me and our children! – to think. They want us to base our behaviour (as individuals and as voters) upon "feelings" and "attitudes" instead. And they want those "feelings" and "attitudes" to be ones which *they* have instilled in us, by various means.

They don't want us to have at our disposal the basic facts upon which we might think to some purpose, either. So they withhold these facts from us, and thus force us to make our judgements in ignorance – whenever they have the power to do so. When they cannot manage this, they try to prevent genuine rational public debate on an issue from arising, so that most of us will not hear both sides of an issue cogently argued.

Who are the Facilitators? They are people in positions of considerable power. Some of them are governing us. Others are "facilitating" us from within the media. Still others are at work in the universities, the civil service, and the "caring" professions. A good many are at work within second-level schools. There are swarms of them.

1

The Facilitators in second-level schools are "facilitating" our children. They seem bent upon altering the attitudes and values of the Irish people in a single generation, so that when the present school generation comes of age, the kind of laws and customs Facilitators favour will be acceptable to the majority.

The changes the Facilitators want are radically unChristian – and yet, curiously, the school Facilitators are being aided and abetted by a host of Catholic educators, including many religious. Most of these Catholic quasi-Facilitators do not want society altered along the lines the Facilitators would choose. But nevertheless, they aid and abet.

Most of this book consists of efforts, by several people, to show the "facilitation" process as it is exercised in Ireland. But before getting down to specifics, we might consider the reasons why Facilitators use their manipulative tactics.

We think they behave thus because they have no respect, philosophically, for the assent to perceived truth which is at the heart of human freedom. They lack this respect because they do not really believe in the rational mind and free will which make such assent possible. They have accepted a conception of the human person which sees man as a mere physical-psychological entity. As a creature who, at best, *can* only be led by emotions: by "feelings", and conditioned "attitudes". A creature who lacks the spiritual capacities of rational thought and free, rationally-guided choice. They therefore see the human person as a fit subject for social engineering.

Why do we call them "Facilitators"? As it happens, we took the word from *them*. In the teaching handbooks our school Facilitators produce (the handbooks containing the attitude-formation programmes they use upon our young) the specially-trained instructors are regularly called "Facilitators", rather than "teachers". Because the "facilitation" game strikes us as much of a muchness whether practised in school or in society at large, we have applied the term to all those who are trying to "facilitate" change by certain manipulative means.

Am I suggesting that these Facilitators belong to some conspiracy? No; not in the least. To see this as a "conspiracy book" would be to miss the point entirely. These Facilitators are not conspirators. Conspirators are people who hide their identities, and most of their intentions, in darkest obscurity. Usually only their fellow-conspirators know who they are. But our Facilitators do not behave thus; they tend rather to court publicity, both for themselves and for their intentions.

And then, conspirators tend to be linked organisationally. A real conspiracy involves some organised hierarchy or network, in which each conspirator takes orders from someone else, up to the level of the top plotters. This is not true of the Facilitators. It is true that many of them belong to certain social-change-promoting organisations – but then, many others do

2

not, and there is no overall organisation to which they all belong.

And conspiracies tend to work by suborning people into cooperation: by threats, bribes, etc. This does not seem to be true of the Facilitators, who give every evidence of acting as they do simply because they sincerely desire certain changes, and hold to a philosophy which does not deter them from using the methods they use.

What unites the Facilitators is simply their shared vision of man and society: their common view of the nature of the human person, and the society proper to persons thus conceived. They are thus a philosophical, rather than a conspiratorial unity. And therefore this book is not an attempt to "unmask a conspiracy", but rather to explain something about the ideas these Facilitators hold, and the kind of behaviour that results from these ideas.

Which means, of course, that we are not saying these Facilitators are "wicked people". Not being able to see inside their minds, we have no idea whether they are wicked or not – and in any case, it is not for us to judge. What we are saying is that they hold a false philosophy of man, and act according to that philosophy. Very often, we can charitably suppose, they do so with the intention of doing good (as they perceive the good) to those they "facilitate".

The distinguishing mark of their philosophy of man seems to be a disbelief in the existence of, or at least a deep disrespect for, the rational mind – especially the rational mind of the ordinary person. (There is a strong strain of élitism in the thinking of the Facilitators.) Some of them – a group busily "facilitating" teenagers down in Cork – have actually produced a handbook for trainee-Facilitators which contains an explicit statement of this debasing philosophy. In that handbook (as you will see in Chapter 2) it is asserted that the rational mind should not be allowed to direct human behaviour. And the "facilitation" programme found in that handbook acts upon this belief with relentless consistency, as you will see when you read our chapters about it.

When seeking a name for the philosophy uniting the Facilitators, we couldn't do better, I think, than adopt Alasdair MacIntyre's word: emotivism. In his brilliant *After Virtue*, Dr. MacIntyre analyses emotivism thus:

> Emotivism is the doctrine that all evaluative judgements and more specifically all moral judgements are *nothing but* expressions of preference, expressions of attitude or feeling, insofar as they are moral and evaluative in character ... (Emotivists hold that) moral judgements, being expressions of attitude or feeling, are neither true nor false; and agreement in moral judgements is not to be secured by any rational method, for there are none. It is to be secured, if at all, by producing non-rational effects on the emotions or attitudes of those

3

who disagree with us (pp.11-12).

I do not mean to suggest that our Facilitators are total theoretical emotivists. Some seem to be; some do not. Many of them have probably never given a thought to the philosophical question involved; and many others may still vaguely perceive themselves as believers in the rational mind and free will, insofar as they think about the matter at all. But still they act as if they were theoretical emotivists, which makes them such for all practical purposes. As Dr. MacIntyre says,

> to a large extent people now think, talk and act *as if* emotivism were true, no matter what their avowed theoretical stand-point may be. Emotivism has become embodied in our culture (p. 21).

Dr. MacIntyre wrote that in another country. Here in Ireland, things have not gone quite that far, perhaps. On this island, emotivism seems so far to be embodied only in the culture of our élite. We live in a society which has become emotivist at the top, but which does not exhibit this form of intellectual degradation at its lower levels. Odd, isn't it? Down among the people – that is, among the "facilitated" and the parents of the "school-facilitated" – most of us still believe that human beings are both able and obliged to act in accordance with what they judge to be right and true when applying certain objective standards. Which is why, perhaps, the Facilitators are so active in schools! They seem to want to make sure the next generation does not emerge from school holding the same "outdated" ideas about the human person, his nature and his duties, as the present one.

In a revealing interview in the *Sunday Tribune* (1 September 1985), Baroness Mary Warnock (who chaired the notorious Warnock Committee which decided that it is morally acceptable to experiment on "spare" human embryos, before – of course! – killing them) told a reporter how she makes her own moral decisions:

> People say – "I *felt* it was the right thing to do, or I just *felt* it was wrong." That's a sound basis for morality . . .

The Baroness' procedure, when making moral choices, is clearly an emotivist one: she consults her sentiments. Like most of us, she finds it difficult to feel sentimental about embryos. Therefore they may, she concludes, be treated like laboratory animals.

The Facilitators want us to learn to make our moral decisions thus. They also tend to favour the same sort of society the Baroness has come to represent: a society which recognises few objective moral norms, but luxuriates in the feeling that it is "caring".

Once we have abandoned the idea that human beings are rational creatures with free wills, meant to be in charge of their own behaviour, we have more or less opted to join the zoo – or worse. We have volunteered ourselves as subjects for the behavioural psychologist's laboratory; we have entered that domain where other non-rational creatures are *trained*: where dogs are conditioned to salivate at the sound of a bell; where panicky rats run about, lost in exitless mazes, while their masters attempt to train them to rodentine obedience. "It is a fact," wrote Alasdair MacIntyre,

> that emotivism entails the obliteration of any genuine distinction between manipulative and non-manipulative social relations. Consider the contrast between, for example, Kantian ethics and emotivism on this point. For Kant – and a parallel point could be made about many earlier moral philosophers – the difference between a human relationship uninformed by morality and one so informed is precisely the difference between one in which each treats the other primarily as a means to his or her ends and one in which each treats the other as an end. To treat anyone else as an end is to offer them what I take to be good reasons for acting in one way rather than another, but to leave it to them to evaluate those reasons. It is to be unwilling to influence another except by reasons which that other he or she judges to be good. It is to appeal to impersonal criteria of the validity of which each rational agent must be his or her own judge. By contrast, to treat someone as a means is to seek to make him or her an instrument of my purposes by adducing whatever influences or considerations will in fact be effective in this or that occasion. The generalisations of the sociology and psychology of persuasion are what I shall need to guide me, not the standards of a normative rationality. (*After Virtue*, pp. 22-23)

When the Facilitators who govern us, or "facilitate" us through the media, attempt to gain our consent to the measures they favour, they characteristically guide themselves by those "generalisations of the sociology and psychology of persuasion", rather than by "the standards of a normative rationality"! If they were guided by the standards of a normative rationality, they would behave quite differently. They would then address themselves to the rational minds of the adult public. They would set forth their aims, and adduce whatever reasons they could to support the claim that these aims were objectively good. They would be far too honourable to conceal from the public those facts which had a bearing upon the matter – but which tended not to support their claims. They would be eager to engage in genuine, free, open debate, conducted according to standard logic, and they would give their opposition every opportunity to put its case, so that truth might more clearly emerge.

When in control of the media, they would be far too decent to take advantage of that control; far too fair-minded to bombard the public hour after hour, day after day, week after week, month after month with incessant propaganda for their aims, interspersed here and there with snide remarks about those who do not share their aims. They would never stoop to trying to cloud the public mind by emotive appeals to such ill-defined concepts as "sectarianism", "divisiveness" and the like. They would not invade the private lives of victims of human weakness, so as to work up public feeling which could then be exploited to produce consent to certain changes in the law or in the legal system.

And they would never attempt to use the schools so as to get other people's children into the habit of making moral choices according to subjective, emotional criteria (supplied by the Facilitators!) rather than according to "the standards of a normative rationality".

Because they are for all practical purposes emotivists, the Facilitators do all of those things. Right now, Irish teenagers are being "facilitated" in several mind-bending "health education" and "lifeskills" programmes in second-level schools. These are not mere "sex education" programmes, although they usually include a unit on sex. They are *complete mental and pyschological formation programmes* designed to alter the whole way young people relate to life. The programmes are designed to alter the young in ways which most Irish parents would indignantly reject – *if they knew what the programmes were like!*

But they *don't* know what they are like; the programmes are kept hidden from them. In some schools, these programmes were in use for two full years, before the parents learned of their existence. And when, having at last become aware of what was being done to their children, parents asked schools and health boards (the health boards prepare the programmes) if they might read the things so as to form their own judgement about whether they were fit for use upon their children, both schools and health boards arrogantly refused. That arrogance, revealing as it does a contempt for the rational minds and free wills of those parents, is characteristic of the emotivist, and thus of the Facilitator. The school Facilitator simply doesn't give a damn what parents think about his "facilitation". As you will see, when you read this book.

Our governing Facilitators showed to what extremes emotivism can carry the powerful, during the campaign preceding the passage of the Pro-Life Amendment. You will discover, later in this book, how they concealed from the public certain basic matters the public *had every right to know*, in order to come to a realistic assessment of what would happen here without that Amendment: what sort of measures this government was prepared to implement. People who guided themselves by "the standards of a normative rationality", rather than "the generalisations of the sociology and psychology of persuasion", would not have behaved thus, we think.

Nor would people who really wanted the public to come to its *own* independent conclusions, according to "the standards of a normative

6

rationality", have attempted to frighten people into voting No, as many Facilitators did during the closing weeks of the campaign. Do you remember the one who told us that so many women might die annually, if the Amendment became law? Do you remember those "This Amendment Will Kill Women" handbills? If that nonsense had been true, we'd have had thousands of funerals by now! Yet those were the tactics used, in order to try to scare us into voting No. They were emotivist tactics: they were devised, apparently, with the intention of "producing certain non-rational effects on the emotions or attitudes".

Toward the end of that campaign (perhaps they were getting a bit panicky?) they lost all their former sophistication, and resorted to simply ordering us, over and over again, to *discard our own rational minds*. Do you remember how they carried on? How they told us that if our rational minds (and our own ability to read simple prose) told us that the Amendment would forbid abortion, whereas the legal mind of our (anti-Amendment) Attorney General told him that it would actually serve to *introduce* it, then we should simply dismiss our own minds, and accept instead the Attorney General's reading of that piece of ordinary prose?

They went on and on that way. Do you remember? In shrill and constant chorus, they more or less shouted: "Don't *try* to read it! Don't trust your own minds! If your mind tells you the thing means the opposite of what Mr. Sutherland says it means, then you must *abandon your mind*! Don't think! Stop! Vote No, or women will *die*!

Would people who respected the rational minds of the electorate have behaved thus? Or does that carry-on bear the mark of the emotivist Facilitator? We leave it to you.

CHAPTER 2

Southern Scene

By the very act of arguing, you awake the patient's reason; and once it is awake, who can forsee the result? Even if a particular train of thought can be twisted so as to end in our favour, you will find that you have been strengthening in your patient the fatal habit of attending to universal issues and withdrawing his attention from the stream of immediate sense experience. Your business is to fix his attention on the stream. Teach him to call it "real life" and don't let him ask what he means by "real".

> —Advice given by Screwtape, a very experienced devil, in C. S. Lewis' *Screwtape Letters*.

On 25 January 1985, the *Independent* carried an odd little article by Gemma Hussey, then our Education Minister. The Minister said that she hoped there would be lots of public discussion about what a national programme in "relationships", education should contain. She also said that in some parts of this Republic, pilot programmes in this area are in use, and that those involved in these "are open to . . . share their experience with others."

She said both of those things, and yet she never *connected* them. She never suggested that interested members of the public buy or borrow the handbooks containing these pilot programmes, study them, and use the knowledge so gained as a basis for their part in her suggested public discussion. Isn't that odd? Why do you suppose the Minister didn't suggest that obvious course of action?

I'll tell you why. She didn't suggest it because the handbooks containing these pilot programmes are *not made publicly available*. Those in charge guard them as if they contained the Star Wars plans, instead of mere directions for giving lessons to teenagers. The "health education" bureaucrats are so bashful about their handbooks that some interested members of the public have been trying unsuccessfully to gain access to the books for over a year. I know, because I am one of those interested members of the public!

True, I now possess several of these handbooks, and I mean to tell you all about one of them soon – but I didn't get it from the bureaucrats behind it, in the Southern Health Board. I got it from a "mole", who sent me the handbook in the post; we call him the "Blessed Mole of Cork", at our house. The North Western Health Board has a similar handbook containing its "Lifeskills Programme", but the bureaucrat in charge won't let us read it.

After he had refused our requests for about a year, we wrote to Mrs. Hussey, asking what she thought of all those refusals – and she supported the bureaucrat completely.

> ". . . whether these materials, or any notes for teachers developed by the project team, should be available to the public is a matter for the Health Board and individual school authorities. I would not propose to intervene and would have to leave this matter to the good sense and judgement of the local school authorities."

The Minister does not think that the public has a natural *right* to read those pilot programmes, which are being used on the public's children. Which makes her call for public discussion sound a bit *hollow*, don't you think?

At this point you may be saying to yourself, "Oh, no! Not *another* article deploring sex education! Do these people never think about anything *else*?" Well, if you are thinking something of that sort, think again – because you have jumped to a false conclusion. Look back to the start of this chapter, please. Did I say anything about sex? Matter of fact, I *didn't*.

Why not? Because these pilot programmes (the ones I've seen, anyway) *are not* "sex education" programmes. They are *total* attitude-formation programmes taking in many areas of life, of which sex is only one. True, the programmes I've read have units on sex. But those units take up only about one-tenth of the allotted time, and those units are no *more* harmful, in my view, than the rest.

These programmes deal with several of the teenagers' important relationships: those with his parents; with his peer-group; with the clergy; with himself. (They omit, significantly, some of his other relationships, such as those with God, with the saints, and with the devil – and these omissions are, I think, a productive subject for speculation.)

In my view, the approach these programmes take to *all* these relationships is harmful to adolescents. Harmful to them as rational and responsible beings, and not merely as sexual beings. These programmes would, I think, have a pernicious effect upon the teenager's *total* self. So please don't think these next chapters are about something called "sex education".

The handbook the Blessed Mole sent me is called *The Social and Health Education Programme: A Handbook for Teachers and Other Educators*. It contains the course which was recognised in 1981 as the official health education programme of the Southern Health Board, which that board offers to schools in cooperation with Ógra Chorcaí – Cork Youth Association. The latest (1982) edition was sponsored by the Southern Health Board and the Cork Trustee Savings Bank. The handbook is a large tome containing a 26-page introductory section outlining the SHB's educational philosophy, followed by 365 pages in which every word and every step of

9

each classroom session is set forth in such explicit detail that anyone reading the handbook knows *exactly* what the entire programme is like.

Which may, perhaps, account for the marked reluctance of these health bureaucrats (and that Minister?) to submit the handbooks to public examination! The SHB calls its teachers "Facilitators" – and I assure you that if I were an SHB Facilitator, and I found that the parents of the teenagers I "facilitated" had my handbook, I'd be mighty nervous. I think I'd be off to Philadelphia in the morning, before those parents started knocking on my door – because the handbook reveals a programme which is based on ideologies, and uses methods, which most Irish parents would indignantly reject. Ideologically, the thing is feminist-permissivist, anti-Catholic, and anti-parent; and in both ideology and method it is profoundly anti-rational. It exalts emotion, peer-group cohesion, and even physiological response (the "sense of touch") at the expense of reason, and it recognises the existence of no objective moral order against which a rational mind might judge principles or actions.

As soon as we open the handbook, this ideology becomes apparent. The Foreword was written by one John Heron, who rejoices in the title of Honorary Co-Director of something which has the monumental – and hugely comic – *hubris* to call itself the "Human Potential Research Project" – located in Guildford, Surrey. Mr. Heron's regard for reason is identical with Screwtape's. "Our educational system," he laments, "rests on an ancient, hierarchical view of the person. In Aristotelian terms, intellect is that which differentiates man from animal . . . In Platonic terms, intellect rules over the nobler emotions, which under the guidance of intellect rule over the baser passions. This authoritarian, hierarchical role anciently ascribed to intellect is with us still today."

O foolish Aristotle! Alas, poor Plato! The Human Potential expert sets them straight:

> The hierarchical, authoritarian model of intellect-in-charge-of-the-person has served its historical and cultural purpose. The time is ripe for an alternative, democratic model: That of co-equal human capacities which mutually support and enhance each other.

For a model, one wonders, in which the rational mind will no longer be seen as distinguishing man from beast? In which the intellect will no longer be in charge of human conduct? In which the baser passions will at last be freed, "democratically", from the tyranny of the guiding mind? Yes. Although Mr. Heron has a few kind words to say about the mind (provided that it does not get above its station and try to *direct* the person!) the class sessions proceed in a way which is explicable only if we assume that these Facilitators *seriously accept* this "democratic model" of the person, and all that it implies. The whole thing rests upon this notion that the judging mind

10

must be *denied* the job of guiding human behaviour, and upon the belief that it is "democratic" thus to submerge the rational capacity.

If we – whose minds, blessedly, have not been formed by Human Potential experts! – break the programme's cardinal rule and *think* about the proposition that human freedom is enhanced by demoting the rational mind to the same level as the glands, we cannot but see that the notion is fatuous. A moment's thought suffices to show that no human being can remain free if he does not use his rational mind to guide his behaviour, because without rational guidance a person must exist at the beck and call of his appetites and emotions. In which state, he would be easy prey for every demagogue and seducer whose path he crossed – because seducers and demagogues are adept at using the fears and desires of others in order to control their behaviour. A person ruled by his appetites and passions would be as helpless before such conditioners as Pavlov's dogs, before the laboratory assistant who rang their dinner-bell. And what of democracy then?

I reflected thus, while reading the handbook the Blessed Mole sent. And gradually, it became clear that this programme is *exactly* what a really up-to-date totalitarian State would choose, in order to condition its young into a habit of immediate and unthinking acceptance of its propaganda and decrees. In every class session, the activities are structured, and the questions and directions phrased, so as to make thoughtful, rational, objectively-grounded responses all but impossible. First, the Facilitators *never ask* the kids to think; they always ask them either to blurt out their feelings, or respond physically to stimuli. And in case the odd thinking teenager tries to squeeze an objective, rational comment into the proceedings, the Facilitators' notes are full of warnings against letting anyone be "judgemental". In this book, "judgemental" is a word of extremely wide meaning. The notes make plain that the Facilitators must condemn as "judgemental" *every act of rational judgement* by which a person considers whether an idea is true or untrue, a form of behaviour right or wrong, or even an object beautiful or ugly. Exercising that sort of judgement is childish and "shallow", they say – whereas surrendering onself to sheer experience is grown-up. Using one's rational mind to decide about something, with the intention of basing action upon that decision, is a thing these Facilitators simply cannot abide.

Therefore, the class sessions are engineered so as to *bypass* the kids' minds; to produce attitudinal and behavioural changes, without any resistance from the rational capacities of those changed. This conditioning starts in the first session which (like all subsequent sessions) induces the kids to obey the Facilitator's instructions instantly and without reflection, even when those directions do violence to their own right to privacy. The exercise presents itself, disarmingly, as a couple of innocent little games. In the first, called "Throwing the Cushion", the kids are arranged in a circle and told to toss a cushion to one another, calling out their names as they do so. After

11

a while (that is, after they have got used to uttering instant and unthinking responses on cue) a new game starts: a kind of psychological "Paul Jones". A record is played, and whenever the music stops the Facilitator reads out the first part of a sentence, which each teenager then has to complete aloud – instantly, and without reflection – to the person he found himself facing when the music stopped. The sentences include these:

"When I can find time to be alone, I like to . . . . ."
"When I first met my closest friend, I . . . . ."
"My fears about this group now are . . . . ."
"One thing about me I would like to change is . . . . ."

Do the kids ever rebel at this point? Do they ever throw the cushion at the Facilitator, and refuse to continue? I'd like to think they do – but suspect they don't. Why? Well, first of all they *are* in school, and kids never feel that free to say "no" in school, even in 1986. Second, the exercise begins by pretending to be only a little game, which would make anyone who resisted look like someone with a hangup. Third, their very embarrassment at the personal questions would render them weak and vulnerable, and thus less able to refuse with dignity and conviction. It's not easy to be strong and resolute, when you are only 15 and trying hard not to blush! And finally, there's the way these Facilitators use language, especially the word "sharing".

Throughout the programme, divulging one's inmost feelings, memories and desires is called "sharing" – which must put considerable moral pressure on the kids. In their experience, "sharing" has normally been linked with Christian charity: with the idea that the rich ought to "share" with the poor; that children are selfish and greedy if they don't "share" their toys with their brothers and sisters. So when the Facilitator asks them to "share", many teenagers must feel morally confused, and therefore submit themselves to these incursions upon their privacy and dignity.

And in this programme, nothing, absolutely *nothing*, is considered too private for "sharing"! For instance, in a session called "Childhood Memories and Sexuality" (pages 239-241) the kids "share" their sexual feelings and memories within 3-person groups. The Facilitators' notes preceding the session give explicit instructions about the make-up of these groups: "It is useful to have a group of mixed sex for this session. When sub-groups are formed these also should be of mixed sex." That means that when the Facilitator tells them to "form groups of three" and "find a private place and get comfortable facing one another", every group will consist either of one boy facing two girls, or one girl facing two boys. As they sit thus, the Facilitator reads the "topics for sharing", including these: "When did you first become aware of your sexuality as a child?". "What memories do you have of: approaching adolescence; menstruation; the growth of facial hair; voice breaking; awareness of sexual feelings; body development (or lack of it)?"

12

That's what "sharing" means, in this programme. It can also mean acting out little plays in which the characters are supposed to represent the parents, brothers and sisters of teenagers in the room, engaged in a family quarrel. There is no area of personal or family privacy into which this "sharing" does not eventually intrude.

The notes do say that "participants have the freedom not to disclose or to disclose only what they feel comfortable with". But the programme clearly puts the onus of refusal on the individual child. Furthermore, the programme does not allow any boy or girl to refuse to join a group at all – which means that even the best intentioned can be made, against their will, to listen to coerced confidences which violate that normal human sense of what reticence accords with human dignity.

Clearly, the programme does not encourage feelings of family loyalty. For these, it seems to be trying to substitute feelings of group cohesion within the class itself, with the kids all fused into a collectivity which is controlled by the Facilitator. The class is fed this idea of "group cohesion". At the close of the first session, they get it in these questions: "Do you feel any different now about your commitment to the group?" "Is sharing important for the development of group cohesion?" "What factors hinder or help sharing in the group?"

After those questions, the Facilitator "asks each participant to consider how he might contribute to the development of a supportive and trusting group climate". The question of whether it is a good thing to submerge oneself in the "group climate" is, of course, never raised. It is assumed that just as "sharing" is a self-evidently good thing, so is "group conhesion" – regardless of what the group does, or what principles it learns to embrace. "Consensus" is all.

The programme takes up two hours of every teenager's school week – week after week, year after year. In some schools the programme is used in the civics slot; in others, it has a slot all to itself. In others, incredibly, it is used in the RE slot. According to the handbook, it is now used in 49 Cork area schools, and several thousand children have been through it. And all the sessions follow the same basic pattern as the first one, starting off with some artfully-contrived gimmick to break down reticence while increasing vulnerability, and proceeding through "sharing" and discussion periods in which subtly-tendentious directions and questions lead the kids gently towards predestined conclusions, without alerting their rational minds. And the end result is to induce conformity with the secularist values of the Facilitators.

But to accomplish this in Ireland, other obstacles besides the kids' own rational minds have to be removed, or at least circumvented: their loyalty to their families, and to the Church. Anyone, whether Devil or Facilitator, who seeks to build a society which is nothing but a mindless collective, recognising no objectively-valid code of conduct, whose ordinary members

13

accept whatever values their opinion-leaders promote, *must* do something about the Church. Therefore, it should not surprise us that throughout the handbook, the Church is presented as a repressive, harshly-authoritarian political structure, bent on temporal domination. And likewise, the Catholic clergy are presented as the agents as that sort of institution: as rigid, harsh, cold and "uncaring"; whereas those who do things the Church say are wrong are routinely presented as compassionate, "caring", trustworthy, freedom-loving and wise.

On pages 299-305 there is an exercise called "Plebiscite in North Hereland" in which the kids are asked to pretend they live in an imaginary country whose population is divided into two groups of different religion. This is the way the groups are described:

> At one time the whole region professed the *Romeccan faith* and acknowledged the spiritual and temporal overlordship of the *Papatullah* in the city of Romecca in Continentia. Six hundred years ago the heretical *Arisixtus Communion* was founded in Incontinentia and this has been the official religion of the Greater Soxian Empire. At that time Hereland remained true to the Romeccan faith and this is still the majority faith on the island. Three hundred years ago groups of Arisixtians broke away to form *Free Senatorian Communities* which are now united in the *Union of Free Senatorians*. This faith is very strong in Jutoutland and has spread into North Hereland, partly through migration, partly through conversion . . . Recently there has been a revival of the political aspects of Romeccanism and most of Continentia is now united under the temporal as well as the spiritual rule of the Papatullah Mixtus VI.

Throughout the programme, the Catholic Church is presented in those terms. Rome is identified with Mecca, and the Pope with those Ayatollahs our papers report as insisting that thieves' hands be cut off, and women stoned if taken in adultery. And likewise, throughout the programme, those who reject Catholicism are presented as free and democratically inclined – that is as "Senatorian". All this is done gradually and indirectly, by constant suggestion, by hints and images (like the image lurking in the word "Papatullah").

I am not suggesting that because the programme is anti-Catholic, it is pro-Protestant, however. Apart from the "Papatullah" session, in which the Protestants are well treated *because* they are opposed to the Catholics, neither Christian believers nor Christian teaching are presented attractively, and a number of exercises are arranged so as to weaken the kids' allegiance to Christian teaching. In one called "What Are My Values?" (pages 23-25) the kids are asked to "clarify their values" by ranking ten items. Each item is meant to stand for a particular value, and the order in which a teenager

14

arranges them is meant to show which values he thinks most important, which least, etc. The items are: "pound note; TV set; aspirin; a liberated woman; a gun; a text book; a bunch of flowers; a Bible; civil rights; car keys."

There is only *one* item there which a Christian believer could use to represent his specifically religious values: that Bible. But notice, the list does not even say "*the* Bible"; it says "*a* Bible", which puts that Bible before the mind primarily as a book, a mere physical object and one of many such. Yet against this object, the kids are meant to rank a human being (that liberated woman) and a noble abstraction (civil rights). How could anyone place a *book*, considered as an object, above either of those? And yet if one ranks that Bible lower down, one has devalued the only thing the exercise gives as representative of Christian faith.

Among Facilitators, this session is of a type known as "values clarification strategies". These were developed by a group of Secular Humanists (Louis Raths; Sidney Simon, *et al.*) belonging to the "humanistic education movement" in America. According to them, these exercises reveal to teenagers what it is that they themselves "really" value, as opposed to what the adults around them (apart from the Facilitators, of course!) want them to value. How many kids would recognise, doing this thing, that the list of objects was rigged so as almost to compel them to devalue their faith? Not many, surely? Especially since they are not given a chance to think about the ranking quietly, and alone. The session is a very crowded one; it insists that after doing the ranking, the kids must scurry about forming sub-groups, electing secretaries, reaching a consensus in each group, and then reporting to the class for more consensus-forming. In all that confusion, not many kids would be able to analyse the list for built-in bias. So a good many would go home very confused, thinking that although they *thought* they were Christians, still they couldn't be, not *really*, because they had been shown "scientifically" that they really weren't! That's what's meant by "clarification". Facilitators use a lot of Newspeak, don't they?

I said earlier that religious people (the Catholic clergy in particular) are regularly presented as harsh, rigid and dictatorial, whereas those who oppose them are seen as benevolent, freedom-loving, etc. In a session called "Conflict of Secular and Religious Demands" (pages 261-263) the kids are told a story about a local committee and a parish priest. The priest, described as "a remarkable man, powerfully built, with shrewd, loveless eyes", is shown as wanting a boy who stole the committee's funds prosecuted, while the layfolk want to show mercy and give the boy a chance for a new life.

The Facilitators present this as a conflict between "religious and secular demands". But *is* it? What is "religious" about wanting a boy prosecuted? That seems quite a "secular" demand to me. And what is "secular" about wanting to show mercy? If the roles had been reversed, the story would have made equally good (or perhaps better) sense. But in this programme, the clergy *have* to be presented as the baddies. In this session, as throughout, the kids are led to see the Church as represented by those who are harsh and bent on punishment, and to identify kindness and compassion with defiance of the Papatullahs, and thus of the Church.

The programme devalues Christian morality as it does the Catholic clergy; throughout, it shows disapproval for those who try to adhere to Christian rules about moral behaviour, and approval for those who don't. There are references to people like the college student (on page 30) who "saved all his tuition money to give to a friend who has to obtain an abortion" (thus linking self-sacrifice and loyalty with approval of abortion), and the woman (page 29) who is "living with a married man but not married to him" and is also a lawyer who "uses her qualifications to defend those in court who could not pay legal fees (thus linking altruism and intelligence with adultery). I'm not saying, of course, that such combinations are impossible; what I want to point out is that in this programme, the "caring" people seem regularly to be those who take a casual attitude toward the Commandments.

This is not accidental. Those who devised this programme really *believe* that the best kind of people do *not* have firm rules about ethical behaviour. On page 137 the ideal person is described as one from whom "integrity, honesty, responsibility, companionship" and "love" all "flow" – why? Because his *self-esteem* is high! Because he

> feels that he matters, that the world is a better place because he is here . . . He is able to ask others for help, but he believes that he can make his own decisions and is his own best resource . . . He doesn't have any firm rules against anything he feels. He accepts himself as human.—

On pages 259-260 we find an exercise called "Clarifying Feelings About Religious Institutions". Near the close of this session, the kids are asked, "Could you say better now what religious beliefs if any are true and important to you?" So presumably, this session is meant to bring them to certain conclusions about the *truth* of Christian *doctrines*. The procedure is very simple: the Facilitator takes a Roman collar, and "in a dramatic manner" places it on the table in the centre of the group. He then "asks the participants to respond, either verbally or non-verbally, to the collar, noting in particular what feelings are aroused". This response is allowed to continue for a time – during which, I imagine, it would grow in intensity.

What would that response be like? Well, let us consider that collar. It is clear from the questions given that the Facilitator want the kids to take the collar as symbolic of the Church, and also of Christian teaching. But is it really a natural symbol for those things? For *doctrine*? Hardly.

Yet it *is* a symbol; it has been used as such, mostly by Christians, for cen-

16

turies. That stiff collar is a natural symbol not for Christian doctrine, but rather for the "strait" (that is, confining) and "narrow" way that leads to God. It is an uncomfortable-looking collar, and it suggests that those who wear it have accepted a way of life which involves considerable self-restraint. As such, it naturally suggests something we all rebel against; something many saints went through years of prayer and struggle, in order to accept. Which is why George Herbert called the following poem "The Collar":

> I struck the board, and cry'd, No more: I will abroad.
>   What, shall I ever sigh and pine?
> My lines and life are free; free as the road,
>   Loose as the winde, as large as store.
>   Shall I be still in suit?
>   Have I no harvest but a thorn
>   To let me bloud, and not restore
> What I have lost with cordiall fruit?
>   Sure there was wine
> Before my tears did drown it;
> Is the yeare only lost to me?
>   Have I no bayes to crown it,
> No flowers, no garlands gay? all blasted,
>   All wasted?
>   Not so, my heart; but there is fruit,
>   And thou has hands.
>   Recover all thy sigh-blown age
> On double pleasures: leave thy cold dispute
> Of what is fit and not; forsake thy cage,
>   Thy rope of sands
> Which pettie thoughts have made; and made to thee
>   Good cable, to enforce and draw,
>   And be thy law,
>   While thou didst wink and wouldst not see.
>   Away: take heed:
>   I will abroad.
> Call in thy death's-head there; tie up thy fears.
>   He that forbears
>   To suit and serve his need
>   Deserves his load.
>
> But as I rav'd and grew more fierce and wilde
>   At every word,
>   Methought I heard one calling, *Childe*:
>   And I reply'd, *My Lord*.

17

In this poem, the saintly poet is doing exactly what the kids are asked to do in this exercise – up to the last four lines. He is using the clerical collar as a symbol of self-restraint, and reacting angrily against the "strait and narrow" confines of the Christian life. (In fact, when he says "Leave thy cold dispute of what is fit and not", he could be expressing the lesson of this programme as a whole!) At the close of the collar session, the class is asked to complete some sentences on paper:

"The way I really feel about the Church is . . ."
"The beliefs from my childhood religion that still make sense to me are . . ."
"To strengthen and deepen my religious beliefs I need to . . ."

That is, they are asked first for their *feelings* (not their thoughts!) about the Church, as those were summoned up during the collar session. Then, *on the basis of those feelings*, they are asked to *select* those *doctrines* which they still accept. The first part of the sentence more or less compels them to make a selection, discarding some beliefs as appropriate only to "childhood". And then (to make the thing seem pious?) they are asked to think about *deepening those beliefs which remain*. After, presumably, some "childish" doctrines have been deleted.

And yet, not one doctrine or belief has been so much as *mentioned*, let alone discussed rationally! The Facilitators do not allow such discussions, as a matter of policy. On page 253, they say:

"It is not a function of this session to teach official religious doctrines. If questions do arise, the facilitator may suggest that these be raised in Religious Doctrine classes."

True, that is said about another session – but anyone who can manage to get a copy of the handbook from a "mole", as I did, will see that nowhere does the thing allow for rational discussion of doctrines; everywhere, everything is based on feeling. Which should not surprise us, really. After all, Mr. Heron's Foreword is most explicit about the programme's refusal to recognise the students as thinking beings.

It is in sessions like these that the programme tries to neutralise, or circumvent, the influence of the Church. I would suspect that it succeeds with many young people. Only those whose faith is particularly strong would be able to resist much of this, surely? Especially if the programme is taught in a Catholic school? And possibly taught *by* a priest, or religious? (And probably by a well-meaning one at that? Someone who assumed the programme was acceptable, because it was introduced to the school by a person who seemed trustworthy?)

If the teenagers' parents had copies of the handbook, of course, things might be rather different! The parents might then descend on the schools and Southern Health Board Offices, in droves, demanding to know what these Facilitators were up to. But alas, the parents do not have the book, and so the Facilitators proceed, bringing their own kind of "enlighten-ment" to the kids; subtly disarranging their attitudes towards themselves, each other, and the Church. It also seems designed to alter their relationship with their own families, particularly with their parents – as I'll try to show next.

CHAPTER 3

Health With Joy

First, perhaps I'd better try to explain just how it is that these Facilitators can feel both called and qualified to engage in what amounts to social engineering. As far as I can make out, they see themselves as obliged to "work for change" in this way, primarily because of their professional role as "health educators". Now, "health education" sounds like a most innocuous activity, does it not? And it was, at first; when it began (in America, mostly) teachers gave lessons in diet (vitamins and green vegetables), elementary hygiene (brushing the teeth up-and-down instead of sideways) and first aid (what to do when a rattlesnake bites you). It was all quite humdrum (in rattlesnake country, anyway!) and there was nothing in it a parent might object to. It just taught the kids the ordinary rules of good health.

But now "health" has been redefined by the "health educators", and this redefinition used to justify incursion by teachers into areas which have little to do with health as we understand it. The handbook defines "health" thus:

> Health in this sense involves continuous movement towards living life more fully, joyfully and productively. It is the process of fulfilling one's potentialities (p. vi).

Because of this all-embracing new definition of "health" they say that the aim of their programme

> is to develop skills such as the ability to understand patterns of communication and relationships within the family . . . to clarify one's values . . . to make freely-chosen decisions; to . . . formulate a personal philosophy; to relate to groups and institutions ranging from the family . . . to national government; to be in control of one's responses to pressures and opportunities (p. viii).

In pursuit of "health" they say they mean to encourage the boys and girls to

> act on their personal values; to perceive and articulate who they want to become; to get to know their own bodies; to develop their sensory awareness; to be aware and find meaning in their own sensuality and sexuality (p. viii).

They see it as part of their job, as "health educators" to help each

20

teenager choose the life-style he finds most appealing:

> It is important for young people to become aware of the alternatives
> that are available . . . They need to realise that life styles can be dif-
> ferent without necessarily being better or worse, and that they do not
> have to accept a particular life style if it is not appealing to them (p.
> 289).

Because they define "health" as *total personal development*, and because
they feel that as specialists in "health" they are equipped to direct this process, they provide a framework of highly-structured classroom exercises (in
which every word the teacher speaks, and every action he takes, is written
down in the handbook) designed to lead the kids to the discovery of their
identities.

But no programme can provide such a framework for self-understanding
and self-development unless its designers have some sort of philosophy of
man in their own minds, surely? And is not the "health educator's" belief
in all of the above (including his own redefinition of "health"!) understandable only if we view these notions as part of some ideology? The Facilitators
say, anyway, that their programme is consistent with the thinking of some
psychologists and educators, including Sidney Simon, a leading figure in the
American "humanistic education movement". Since these devisers admit
that their programme fits in with the thinking of Dr. Simon, I don't think
we would be unfair to suspect that the "humanistic" philosophy of man
might be implicit in the framework provided, in which the kids are expected
to choose the values they will live by, and the life-styles they will pursue,
as they seek to become "healthy".

Now, not many Irish parents are likely to subscribe to the same
philosophy of man as Dr. Simon and his colleagues. In designing a programme along the lines the "humanistic education movement" would
advocate, the Facilitators have set themselves rather a pretty problem;
somehow, they have to deal with the fact that the kids' parents are sure to
be trying to inculcate values, habits and so forth which would *run counter*
to those of Dr. Simon and his colleagues. In this chapter, then, I'll try to
show how the programme deals with this problem.

Parents (and the kids' families in general) are mentioned frequently. The
teenagers are repeatedly made to discuss their family problems; to make
collages of pipe-cleaner "sculptures" which reveal the emotional interaction within their families; to discuss their parents' attitudes towards
nudity, discussion of sexual matters, etc.

One exercise concerned with family life – "Those Significant Others"
(pages 169-172) – is meant to help the kids answer such questions as:

Who are the significant others in my life and what do they expect of

21

me? What am I willing to give, to commit myself to, privately or publicly?

That is, the exercise is

designed to highlight the conflict . . . between the kind of person I would like to be and the kind of person I think other people expect me to be. Because of their expectations and demands on me, significant people in my life manage to transmit to me how they want me to behave, perhaps what friends they want me to have and so on. Many of these "wants" may coincide with expectations I also have of myself, but some may be unacceptable. In the second part of the session, the focus is on exploring my behavioural response to unreal expectations and demands made by others.

In order to decide which "demands" he is willing to comply with, and which he regards as "unreal" and "unacceptable", each teenager is given a worksheet bearing a heart-shaped diagram, with "ME" at the centre of his heart. The Facilitator tells the kids to write the names of their "significant others" in the appropriate spaces, and under each name to list

three things each of these significant others want you to value. Essentially, what demands do they place on you? What do they want you to be, to do, or to think?

Having done that, the teenager is told to

underline each item that you yourself also value. Now, make a list in the ME box that restates those things you are willing to accept as things you value yourself.

After this, the kids are told to consider the "demands" they find "unreal" and ask themselves these questions:

How do I recognise these expectations? Are they subtle, explicit, demanded, or asked for in a clear and easy way? How do you deal with this discrepancy between what you want for yourself - your values - and what others want for you?

The second part of the session teaches the kids exactly how to say "No" when their "significant others" make "unreal demands" upon them. Quite a lot of time is devoted to this lesson. First, the Facilitator demonstrates the art of refusal; next, the kids are paired off to practise saying "No"; as the handbook puts it, each one picks a situation in which they will want to say "no" in the future, for example the situation in which the unreal demand they thought of in Part I is being made of them.

And afterwards, the whole class practises the same thing over again:

Do a role play in which various members of the . . . class act the parts of the significant others in your life, stating the expectations they have of you and the values they want you to hold. You also state the values and aspirations which you hold. Try to become aware of the extent to which they differ and what you would like to do about this.

The next session, on pages 173-175, is called "Negative Criticism". The notes suggest that only criticism based on emotion is acceptable:

You have a right to request a change in another's behaviour if it hurts, irritates or upsets you . . . On the other hand labelling the other with such epithets as "you're selfish" can undermine a person's self-esteem and is unhelpful in producing change.

So any criticism based on a genuine attempt to evaluate behaviour by an objective standard is unacceptable, whereas it is perfectly acceptable to say, "stop criticising me! You are lowering my self-esteem!"

Three classes later (pages 185-188) there is a session called "Family Quarrel". Am I being unfair if I suspect that this session comes in here because the previous sessions would be bound to provoke a good few family quarrels? Whatever the cause, the Facilitators now provide a lesson in how a teenager can handle family quarrels, without surrendering to any "unreal demands". The kids are told that when families quarrel, the antagonists play certain roles, and the names of these roles are "avoiding", "placating", "blaming", and "preaching".

All these roles put pressure on others to respond in certain ways. They are all means of avoiding honest contact, ways of not openly declaring and taking responsibility for what an individual wants from others.

Four teenagers are chosen to act the parts of four family members, quarrelling. Each one plays each "manipulative role" in turn:

To start, let the "Mother" play the placating role, the "Father" play the avoiding role, the "Son" play the blaming role and the "Daughter" the preaching role.

They all switch roles four times, and at the end the "Mother" is

23

"preaching" while the "Daughter" is "blaming". After the "role play" come the questions:

> Did this improvisation make you any more aware of the types of manipulative roles played by you and other members of your family? . . . Do you think that this session will be of any help in recognising when someone else is trying to manipulate or pressurise you?

This session ignores the fact that parents are adults, with a responsibility to guide their children. It quite relentlessly places all family members on the same level of authority, and makes a point of demonstrating that their "roles" are to be regarded as interchangeable.

An earlier exercise, called "Conflict of Rights" (pp. 79-81) also illustrates the Facilitators' perception of human conflict. Here, the kids are paired off and lined up facing one another, with a good bit of space between. Then the partners are told to walk directly toward one another until they meet, when

> one or other of you will have to either back up or step aside . . . The person who does this is indicating weakness of will or lack of concern for personal freedom.

The partners, at that point, are supposed to try to resolve the situation – but they are *not allowed to speak to each other*. The exercise is meant to teach the non-violent resolution of conflicts, yet it insists that conflicts should be resolved *without* rational debate. First, it sets up a situation (as a model of the "conflicts of rights"!) in which, objectively, no real rights (or wrongs) can exist at all, because all that is at stake is the "right" to walk straight across a room. And then, it forbids discussion, and suggests that the way to resolve this conflict (and so, presumably, most conflicts?) is for each party to give in a bit, so that a consensus is reached:

> This coming week, notice when you find yourself in this type of conflict situation, notice how you handle the situation – do you give in? compromise? opt out, go into "temper tantrum", or do you listen, and try to reason it out, try to hear others' views, reach a consensus?

When they speak here of "reason" they clearly do not mean that people should measure the different views against an objective standard, to decide what is right and what is wrong. What they mean is that in every conflict, it is best to reach a compromise solution, which is acceptable to most people. The person who is unwilling to go along with the consensus position is presented as one who goes in for "temper tantrums" or who "opts out".

Now, this "consensus" approach is fine for situations involving no more

24

than a "right" to walk across a room. It is fine in any conflict which is a matter of opposed wills alone; any conflict in which a serious moral issue is not at stake. As subjectivists, these people do not seem able to conceive of conflict situations involving issues which, for those of us who accept an objective moral order, cannot be resolved by an appeal to "consensus".

Discussions of family difficulties, as staged by the Facilitators, appeal to feeling alone, and recognise no objective moral order. And they are staged in the classroom, which means that the kids' problems are being discussed by people those teenagers have not freely chosen to consult.

Yes, the kids are told that they need not reveal their feelings and experiences, now and then. But the sessions are so arranged that a teenager who wanted to keep his private affairs private would appear unco-operative, would stand out from the rest, and might even feel guilty. And even if a young person had enough moral fibre and family loyalty to refuse to criticise his own family, he would still be forced to listen to the other kids betraying the private concerns of their families. He would become, in a way an "accessory after the fact".

If the teenager who refused to reveal his own parents' shortcomings was nevertheless aware that his parents were not perfect, what would go on inside him as he watched his classmates performing on cue? Might not his natural resentments spill over on to his family anyway, if he felt that his parents' faults resembled those of the other kids' parents? And, as the teacher (perhaps a nun!) obviously agreed with the kids who were telling the class how "unreal" their parents were, might not even the reticent teenager be tempted to indulge his resentments?

This whole programme, you will recall, is one of those pilot programmes which Gemma Hussey enthused about in her *Independent* article; that is, it seems to be a prototype for the "relationships education" programme now being prepared by the Health Education Bureau, for national use. So, how do Facilitators deal with sex, in this pilot programme? I'll try to show how, in what follows, which is based on the nine-session sex unit on pages 217-247, entitled "Sensory Awareness and Sexual Identity".

The unit has a preface, containing the Facilitators' justification for this unit. I myself am unable to decide how seriously to take it. What follows is a faithful paraphrase of their argument; it is not a parody.

(1) There is "a huge difference between sensuousness and sexuality";
(2) A teenager can be taught "that satisfying the need for physical contact does not necessarily entail sexual contact";
(3) "Our culture does not place a high value on sensory awareness" which devaluation turns us into "inhibited" and "alienated" individuals;
(4) Therefore it is urgently necessary that schools embark on programmes *to teach sensuality* which will involve breaking down "repressive" Irish "cultural inhibitions" and "taboos"; because

25

(5) The kids thus sensualised will be better able to *resist* pressures toward "premature sexual relationships"!

That's it; cultivation of *sensuality* is supposed to keep the kids away from "premature" (whatever that means) *sexual* activity! After this bit, the Facilitators then leave "innocent sensuality" and get on to the "hugely different" subject of sex – at which point they seem to get a bit confused, because they say, "Since sexuality is a part of the sensuous life, the sessions on sensory awareness should provide a useful foundation for the sessions on sexual identity." Ah, yes; of course! The two things are *hugely* different, chalk and cheese really – but still, the one naturally provides a foundation for the other!

About sex, they say that Irish culture is inhibiting; that this culturally-induced inhibition makes wrecks of Irish adults; and that therefore the kids must be encouraged "to examine and re-evaluate their attitudes towards their sexuality", presumably to avoid being inhibited. To buttress this up, they quote from Virginia Satir, on the horrible consequences of sexual inhibition:

> If you had seen as much pain as I have that clearly resulted from inhuman and repressive attitudes about sex, you would turn yourselves inside out immediately to change your whole attitude to one of open acceptance, pride, enjoyment . . .

The unit does not, by the way, include any factual information on the biology of sex. The preface says that "there is a certain amount of resource material" about this in the Ógra Chorcaí office, should a Facilitator require it, but the material is not in the bound copy of the book the Blessed Mole sent me. The unit, as it appears in the book, is devoted entirely to *changing the kids' attitudes*, rather than enlightening their minds.

The first four sessions are lessons in sensuality. When I write thus, I am not accusing the Facilitators of something they are shy about admitting themselves, remember! They are very explicit about their intention to "awaken the senses", and pay particular attention to awakening the "sense of touch" because that sense "has become the object of strong cultural taboo". This means, they want to "educate" the kids' *skins*. They also want to awaken the other senses "sight, smell, taste, hearing". But they do *not* mean by this that they want the young people to become more aware, aesthetically, of the beauty of the natural world. They pour scorn on aesthetics:

> Our perception is very much narrowed if we feel a need to make judgements about or to label an object; to decide if something is beautiful or ugly, good or bad, useful or useless. Such evaluations are

shallow compared to the reality of the actual objects as touched, tasted, seen, heard, or smelled.

In other words, a happy pig rolling about in a dungheap is experiencing the world properly, whereas poor old Plato, writing about the Good, the True, and the Beautiful, was "shallow"! As always, the Facilitators want to keep the *mind* out of things.

The first session in this unit is called "Let's Use All Our Senses" pages 217-219). First, the kids are asked to walk around the room, eyes closed, trying to be as sensually aware as possible of everything they touch:

Explore this room with all parts of your body, your feet for example are extremely sensitive, your face can be exquisitely sensitive. Keep your eyes closed to accentuate perception by touch . . . How sensitive is the back of your hand or the sole of your foot? How does something feel when it rests against your abdomen, or when you feel it against your thighs?

In the next session, the kids are asked to get into sensual contact with some rocks. Each one gets a rock, and he is told to

feel the surface of the rock over your face . . . Experience its temperature, its texture . . . Put your lips against the rock . . . Where are the differences in its contours? Taste the rock . . . Smell it . . .

Then, after all the tasting and smelling and fingering of contours, they are asked these questions:

How did it feel to perceive the rock with all your senses? How would it feel, do you think, to be known like that by another person, to have another person be totally sensitive to you?

That is, the Facilitator asks them to imagine how it would feel to *change places* with one of those rocks – the same rocks they have been stroking, caressing, smelling and tasting for the last 20 minutes or so. If these Facilitators really think that exercise in imagination is going to keep the kids from "premature sexual relationships", then those Facilitators must think Irish teenagers extraordinarily non-combustible.

The next session, called "Awareness of Self" (pages 225-228) introduces them to the delights of touching their own bodies, in order to become more "creative". "Touching oneself," the notes say, "can sensitise oneself to one's body and can lead to appreciation and celebration of one's uniqueness." The session is performed to music, the notes continue, because "music is useful for disrupting old habits and inhibitions . . . It is impor-

27

tant . . . to have music which is stimulating and expressive''. This attack on "inhibitions" is necessary, the notes say, because there is "a cultural taboo against touching oneself.'' So the kids are asked to put on blindfolds, lie on the floor, and start touching various parts of their bodies; to put a hand on one's "chest, and focus on the sensation . . . As you proceed, you are likely to find it easier to let yourself go and enjoy the fascination of your body.''

What are we to make of all that? Of course, the Facilitator only suggests they touch their chests, brows, noses, etc, and not other parts of their adolescent anatomies. This is only a lesson in "creative" sensuality, and has *nothing whatever* to do with sex, and anyone who thinks it might just has a nasty mind, so there! This is the third session in the unit, but so far the Facilitator has not once breathed the word "sex" to the class. There's plenty about it in the Facilitator's notes, but nothing in what the Facilitators are meant to say to the kids, who are only told they are exploring innocent sensuousness, in order to be more "alive" and "creative".

The next session, called "Caring and Communicating Non-Verbally" (pages 229-231) is still not supposed to be sexual, although it has the kids paired off (I think we can assume in boy-girl pairs?) and giving each other little hand-squeezes and caresses, to "communicate non-verbally". The Facilitator tells them to close their eyes, and explore their partner's hands ("feel the texture, the shape; explore the fingers") and then try to communicate various emotions through their hands alone – especially "caring" emotions. After this, they are arranged in a circle, and told to massage each other's necks and shoulders for a while, after which they are sat down and asked such questions as these:

"Was it difficult to let go and enjoy the massage?"
"Did you feel a sense of being cared for, relaxed, soothed?"
"What connection, if any, do you see between caring and touching and sexual interaction?"
"Is it acceptable in our culture to touch others?"
"Is it easy to communicate caring for others in this way?"
"Can you remember times in your life when you were held and given nurturance by someone and felt you were cared for; could we increase this kind of caring in our lives? How?"

What do you think of all that? Myself, I find it woefully wrongheaded, deceptive and naive. I think it *wrongheaded* because in it the Facilitators assume that an enormous amount of essentially human communication can be conducted through the "sense of touch" alone, when in fact the only things we can communicate that way are a few very basic emotions, and ones that are not exclusive to human beings at that. If we want to communicate in a way which is truly *human*, we must use a good deal more than

28

that "sense of touch".

This exercise is *deceptive* because it contains the hidden assumption that those we care for will understand our "caring" best if we touch, hold and fondle them. Which is, when we stop to consider it, manifestly untrue! Take, for example, a teenage boy's "caring" relationship to a neighbour. Not, in this case, a young, attractive, nubile neighbour of the opposite sex, but an old, half-blind and rather crotchety neighbour instead. If that teenager really cares for this neighbour, will he show it by Ógra Chorcaí-type fondling? Or by demonstrating a steady willingness to do things like read the local paper aloud, or do messages for him? That sort of "caring" may not be quite as pleasurable as the other sort – but it is "caring" all the same. It is moreover, a kind of "caring" which is not in such abundant supply in this fallen world as the sort we show by cuddling those we find physically attractive.

This Ógra Chorcaí line on communicating by the "sense of touch" is also *naive*, I think, in that it is based on the assumption that whenever a person (a teenage boy, for example?) tries to hold, touch, caress and fondle another person (like a teenage girl, maybe?) he acts this way because he wants to demonstrate his "caring" for her. Is it horribly cynical of me – or is it merely realistic? – to wish that *somewhere* in this wretched course the Facilitators had *just once* pointed out that alas, sometimes boys have less "caring" intentions toward the girls they try to fondle?

Which brings me to another highly curious fact about this sex unit: it never once acknowledges the *existence* of sexual desire; it never once adverts to that well-known phenomenon. It is simply chock full of things (innuendoes, little games, etc.) which would be likely to lead people into situations where such desire would be aroused, yet it never once admits, in so many words, that human beings can want one another sexually. Instead, it constantly suggests that those activities we see as connected with sex are somehow not really sexual at all.

Those, then, are the softening up sessions. After these, sex comes out of the closet as the group moves on to the one called "The Language of Sexuality". This is an old favourite with the International Planned Parenthood Federation, and has been found useful in breaking down "taboos" in many countries. The kids are asked to say all the words they can think of for the sexual acts and organs. The book says this exercise is meant to "increase our ease in talking about sex in a group", and also that it "gives an opportunity for the correction of some frequently-encountered mis-understandings".

No doubt those who devised this course would say I am being prudish, "inhibited" and the rest of it, if I said that there is something about this which makes me uneasy. No doubt they would say, in very righteous voices, that there is "nothing sinful about using certain 'taboo' words", and so on. And on course there isn't anything sinful, strictly speaking, in the mere use of a word.

But all the same, I think that there is a subtle change which takes place in a person when he begins to feel at ease using this language, or speaking about intimate matters in a group – especially a mixed group. I think this exercise is *designed to effect that change*; and I think that those who have so changed will then have lost an important natural protection against sexual exploitation. You may call this protection an "inhibition" or a "taboo" if you choose – but the fact remains that it serves a useful function in any society which values chastity.

The sixth session in the unit, called "Sexual Values Clarification", involves two fictional stories about fornication. In each, the woman agrees to sexual intercourse with a third man, in exchange for transport to visit her lover. It is not made explicit, but seems assumed, that the original pair are "lovers' in the full sense: that is, that they have already been fornicating for some time on a regular basis. One couple is presented as engaged, and the other merely as "lovers".

A story is read, and then the kids are asked to rank the characters according to which they "liked best" and "liked least". That is, according to mere personal preference; it is *not* suggested that any moral criteria might be applicable. Nowhere in the discussion is the fact that the lovers are not married mentioned; the fact that they are unmarried is treated as irrelevant. As for the woman's fornication with the other man, the possibility that she might say, "All right then; I'll stay home" is never considered. A desire to visit one's lover is treated as having such overriding importance that one would naturally consider the suggested bargain seriously. One of the discussion questions is "What would you want of a friend if you were in this type of dilemma?" The Facilitators see the alternatives presented to the woman as amounting to a *real dilemma*, in which a friend's advice would be required to find a good answer. After the discussion questions, the Facilitator

> invites participants to consider how their attitudes might have changed as a result of this session and how that might affect their future behaviour.

I invite you to consider the same!

The seventh session is the one in which the kids "share" their sexual memories, already mentioned. The eighth, called "What Are My Priorities?" (pages 243-244) asks the class to list eight things they "value in a sexual relationship". The Facilitator doesn't explain precisely what is meant by a "sexual relationship", but by this time I imagine the kids would be pretty sure that it means a relationship involving some form of highly erotic lovemaking. If so, how would those teenagers who had not yet embarked on such relationships feel, when asked to make their lists? The

30

assignment, after all, *presumes* that they know enough about "sexual relationships" to list the things they value in them! Wouldn't the ones who
hadn't had any such relationships feel left out, perhaps almost *retarded*?
And then what?

The ninth exercise, called "Couple Relationships" (pages 245-247)
involves things "a couple in a long standing relationship" might disagree
about. This time (for the *first* time in the unit) the handbook acknowledges
that there is, in fact, something called "marriage" – but it does not, of
course, *endorse* that arrangement as having any particular value. The
session involves a worksheet, supposed to help couples in "negotiating on
different aspects of a relationship". The questions are about things like
where they want to live (city or country); what sort of jobs they want; how
much time they want to spend together; how each one can "grow as a
person", etc. The sheet is meant to help the partners "resolve conflicts and
achieve harmony by negotiating a position both partners can agree upon".
Any solution which both can agree upon is regarded, by the Facilitators, as
acceptable; consensus is all. The worksheet includes this set of questions:
"To what extent do I want to be sexually involved?"
"Do I want to say no to any sexual interaction?"
"Do I want to wait until I feel ready for such interaction – e.g. until I'm
more mature, more able to handle relationships, until I'm married?"

Those last words, presented as one of several *equally acceptable*
possibilities, are the *sole reference* to marriage in the entire sex unit. Which
should not surprise us, really; the whole programme is, after all, built upon
the notion that emotion, peer-group solidarity, and even sensual appetites
should be "democratically" allowed as much of a role in determining
human decisions as the rational mind – and the idea that sex should be
reserved for marriage is a very rational idea, which is not readily
appreciable unless the mind is allowed the upper hand.

For that matter, every time we attempt to decide what we *should* do, in
any situation, rather than what we merely *want* (emotionally, physically) to
do, we are engaged in a rational exercise; we are using our judgmental
capacities to measure proposed courses of action against an objective moral
standard. Which exercise the Facilitators thoroughly disapprove of! They
feel that an objective moral standard is something imposed from outside an
individual to restrict his freedom, and that therefore an individual who
weighs his conduct against such a standard is not "responsible" for himself,
because he is obeying something "external":

> Frequently the behaviour of others is used as a guideline in determining
> an answer to the question, "What should I do?" To change this
> question and ask "What do I want to do?" implies switching the
> motivation for behaviour from external control to internal control
> (responsible individual choice).

Thus they dispose of the Commandments as well as of several millenia of philosophical enquiry in the realm of ethics: no one need have bothered. All we ever need do is say, "I *want* to", and that's that; all moral problems are dissolved. It's really *thorough*, this little course. It disposes of everything human beings have ever "scorned delights and lived laborious days" for; *everything*. Only the naked will of the individual asserting what he WANTS is recognised.

In the sort of world the Facilitators seem bent on facilitating, *civilisation itself* would simply have to die. It would be like the end of the *Dunciad*:

Art after art goes out, and all is night.
See skulking Truth to her old cavern fled,
Mountains of casuistry heap'd o'er her head!
Philosophy, that lean'd on Heaven before,
Shrinks to her second cause, and is no more.
Physic of Metaphysic begs defence,
And Metaphysic calls for aid on sense! . . .
Religion blushing veils her sacred fires,
And unawares Morality expires . . .
Lo! thy dread empire, Chaos! is restor'd;
Light dies before thy uncreating word;
Thy hand, great Anarch! lets the curtain fall
And universal darkness buries all.

But that sort of chaotic situation wouldn't last long, of course. Sooner or later, those who were more clever and/or ruthless than the rest of mankind would learn to control their fellows – even as the Facilitators control the teenagers in this programme. The programme's theories would produce chaos; but all through the programme the Facilitators themselves stand above their theories, as they stand above the children. It would be the same in any society, in which men had learned to despise what the programme teaches our young to despise: first society would disintegrate into chaos, and then society's Facilitators would move in, and impose their will upon the rest – a process which C. S. Lewis made clear, in this passage from *Christian Reflections*:

Until modern times no thinker of the first rank ever doubted that our judgements of value were rational judgements or that what they discovered was objective. It was taken for granted that in temptation passion was opposed, not to some sentiment, but to reason. Thus Plato thought, thus Aristotle, thus Hooker, Butler and Doctor Johnson. The modern view is very different. It does not believe that value judgements are really judgements at all. They are sentiments, or complexes, or attitudes, produced in a community by the pressures of environment

32

and its traditions, and differing from one community to another. To say that a thing is good is merely to express our feeling about it; and our feeling about it is the feeling we have been socially conditioned to have.

But if this is so, then we might have been conditioned to feel otherwise. "Perhaps", thinks the reformer or the education expert, "it would be better if we were. Let us improve our morality". Out of this apparently innocent idea comes . . . the fatal superstition that men can create values, that a community can choose its "ideology" as men choose their clothes . . .

Many a popular "planner" on a democratic platform, many a mild-eyed scientist in a democratic laboratory means, in the last resort, just what the Fascist means. He believes that "good" means whatever men are conditioned to approve. He believes that it is the function of him and his kind to condition men; to create consciences by eugenics, psychological manipulation of infants, state education and mass propaganda. Because he is confused, he does not yet fully realise that those who create conscience cannot be subject to conscience themselves. But he must awake to the logic of his position sooner or later; and when he does, what barrier remains between us and the final division of our race into a few conditioners who stand themselves outside morality and the many conditioned in whom such morality as the experts choose is produced at the experts' pleasure? The very idea of freedom presupposes some objective moral law which overarches rulers and ruled alike. Subjectivism about values is eternally incompatible with democracy. We and our rulers are of one kind only so long as we are subject to one law. But if there is no law of nature, the *ethos* of any society is the creation of its rulers, educators, and conditioners; and every creator stands above and outside his own creation.

CHAPTER 4

From Whence It Spawns

The programme described in the previous two chapters is used in about 50 second-level schools in Co. Cork. Another emotivist programme of this general type, the North Western Health Board's "Lifeskills Programme for Schools", is used in every second-level school in Counties Sligo, Leitrim and Donegal. Still other programmes designed to "facilitate" children into forsaking the standards of a normative rationality are springing up all over the country – like toadstools. From whence do they spawn?

The centre of contagion appears to be the Health Education Bureau in Dublin, an organ of our Department of Health. The HEB runs a teacher-training programme designed to turn ordinary teachers into Facilitators. Once trained, each new Facilitator is then expected to devise, implement and "facilitate" his own programme in the school where he is employed. Thus, the thing is meant to *multiply*. If the HEB's plans succeed, we may in a few years be faced with as many "facilitation" programmes as there are schools. Like the Gadarene devils, their name will be legion.

Why is the HEB encouraging this multitude of not-quite-identical programmes, instead of simply producing one standard programme of its own for use in all schools? The answer is obvious: if the HEB produced only one programme, some "Blessed Mole" would soon "leak" it to people like us. We would publish our analyses of it and presently, public debate might blessedly arise. As a result of hearing both sides of that debate, many parents would decide the programme was unfit for use upon human beings.

However if each school runs its *own* programme (as devised by a Facilitator trained by the HEB) it will be impossible for people like us to obtain and analyse them all. And therefore, each school will be able to claim that its programme is nothing like the ones which have been analysed. Parents would not know what to believe, in such confusion. So clearly, it is in the Facilitators' interest that a multiplicity of these programmes exist.

However, we at least possess a copy of the HEB's own teacher-training progamme (sent by another "Blessed Mole", of course!) which I have duly photocopied and sent to the Central Catholic Library (74 Merrion Square, Dublin 2) for its "Unspeakable File".

If you betake yourself to that library to read this thing, you will observe that it is contained in a loose-leaf volume of some 200 pages, consisting mostly of classroom exercises and questionnaires and ending with an unpaged bibliography and "resources" list. It bears the title, *Teacher Training Programme in Health Education.* When you read the Introduction, you will note (page 5) that the HEB does not expect *you* to be reading its handbook. This manual it says, "is supplied *only* to participants of the

34

course" (my emphasis).

If you compare this book with the Ógra Chorcaí handbook, you will observe a strong family resemblance, and some omissions. The Cork handbook contains the sort of programme Facilitators want given to the *teenagers* whose attitudes and feelings on religion, family life, and sexuality they want to change. It therefore includes units about those specific topics, as well as lots of material apparently designed to engender a subjectivistic and morally-relativistic view of life.

The HEB programme is meant for use on *teachers* who will have ready access, once trained, to any number of classroom exercises about family life, religion, or sex. Therefore, the HEB programme does not contain units on those specific topics, but devotes itself entirely to providing its trainees with an emotivist approach to use when dealing with such topics. Thus, we read in the Introduction (page 5) that the programme

> aims at equipping teachers with basic training in the skills strategies and methodologies to devise, introduce and facilitate programmes in post-primary schools . . . after training, teachers ought to have the flexibility and confidence needed to devise, adapt and utilise health education materials and resources from whatever source for their school programmes.

If your children will be attending second-level schools in the near future, it is unlikely that you will be able to avoid the "health education" problem. In all likelihood, your children's school will offer a programme devised, introduced and "facilitated" by some HEB-trained Facilitator. What will this programme deal with? Why, with "health", of course! But for HEB-trained Facilitators, "health" is an all-inclusive term – so that programme will include a number of subjects which are not really part of *health* (in the normal sense of the word) at all, but which really belong in ethics and religion. In fact, if the programme your kids are faced with is typical, it will devote *most* of its time to such topics. In its own characteristic way! That the HEB intends its trained Facilitators to deal with moral and religious matters is made abundantly clear in the manual. For instance, it says on page 9 that a

> balanced health education curriculum must be aimed at the whole person and his total health – physical, emotional, social and spiritual.

The manual gives the trainees a list of "health education concerns" which they are clearly meant to include in the programmes they devise. This list (page 169) includes the following topics: "morality"; "family living"; "responsibility"; "sex education"; "relationships"; and "death".

When you discover that your child's school is giving the kids such a pro-

35

gramme (and you may find out rather late in the game; in two Sligo schools, parents only discovered their kids were getting "Lifeskills" two years too late!) I would advise you to do two things, *immediately*. First, tell the school that you do *not* want your child in that class until you have read the *entire* programme and *all* materials connected with it. That is, until you have read those things in *your own home*; until you have photocopied all the parts relating to moral choice; until you have shown those photocopies to whomever you want and taken advice from anyone you choose; and until you are thoroughly satisfied that the programme approaches these topics *exactly* as *you* want them approached.

When I say "moral choice", by the way, I am *not* thinking merely, or even primarily, about sex! These are *not* mere "sex education" programmes. They are *total* mind-formation programmes, which (as you saw in the Ógra Chorcaí chapters) attempt to form attitudes and inculcate feelings on the entire gamut of moral behaviour. So please, don't start reading the thing (if you can get your hands on it) with *only* sex in mind. Your child's programme may not in fact deal directly with sex, or it may not begin dealing with it until the kids have been in the programme for several years. The sex part may not be written yet.

If the school lets you read the thing (which is unlikely; many schools do everything they can to *avoid* letting parents read these materials) you must then analyse it. Now this *can* be confusing, at first – as I know from experience! It is easy to miss the harmfulness of these things, especially on a quick reading. (Which may be why so many schools, if they allow the parents to look at the programme at all, insist that the reading be done in the school – and probably under some Facilitator's eye!) This is because the programmes are not at all frank about stating the philosophy upon which they are based. The programmes *are* emotivist programmes which teach relativism and subjectivism – yet they don't *say* so, clearly and plainly. But really; would you *expect* them to, under the circumstances?

The Facilitators never come right out and say, in plain words, that they do not believe in an objective standard of morality. They do not make unequivocal emotivist assertions such as "Words like 'good' and 'true' have no objective meaning, but are only expressions of feeling or culturally-conditioned attitudes." If you comb your child's programme for explicit statements of that sort, you won't find them – unless the Facilitator who wrote it is remarkably clumsy. The programmes induce the kids to *accept* precisely those ideas – but they do so quite subtly, without stating those ideas in clear and open language. So you have to know just what clues to look for, when you start reading that programme.

What sort of fine-tooth comb do you require, if you want to find out what this programme is really up to? My advice is to start out by concentrating your attention, not so much on what the programme *says*, as on what it leaves *out*.

36

First, decide what the exercise or unit you are reading is really *about*. That is, work out what the subject-matter is, when translated into *your* language, and out of "Facilitationese". For instance, if the book says the exercise is meant to teach the "skills of decision-making" and then gives the kids *moral* conundrums to practise those "skills" on, the exercise is really about moral choice – regardless of that your child's Facilitator has *called* it.

That's your first step. Your second step is to put the handbook aside, and work out what *you* want *your* kids to have in mind when they are making moral choices. What questions do you think a person *should* ask himself, when he is deciding whether to tell a lie or not? Whether to pass on some choice piece of cruel gossip? Whether to join the Women's Right to Choose Group?

You will probably find that you want your kids to have *moral* criteria in mind when they make such moral choices! You want them to ask themselves which choice is objectively *right*, and which is objectively *wrong*. You want them to ask themselves whether one choice is more in line with objective truth than another.

Then go back and look at the exercise or unit, to see if it asks the kids to bear in mind what *you* think people should bear in mind when making moral choices. If the programme follows the HEB model, it *won't*! If it follows the HEB model, it will do everything possible to induce your child to make moral choices *without* reference to moral criteria. It will read as if the devising Facilitator wants kids to make moral choices in a moral void, according to criteria which have nothing to do with objective morality.

It will provide lots of questions for your child to ask himself, when confronted with a moral choice. And those questions may not sound so bad – at first. Each one of them, taken individually, may sound perfectly all right – so much so that if you had approached the programme without first working out what you think people *should* have in mind during such decisions, you mightn't have noticed much wrong. But if you have worked out what *should* be there, you'll be forcibly struck by its absence.

This absence will show up even in vocabulary. The programme will avoid words like "right" and "wrong", "true" and "false" as if they carried some deadly contagion. It will employ the most stilted language at times, in its efforts to speak about moral choices without using such words – and after a while, you may find yourself laughing, in a wry sort of way, at these devious circumlocutions! The programme will go on about choosing the most "rewarding" or "attractive" or "desirable" alternative. The kids will be asked to think about which choice is most "appropriate". They will *never* be asked to think about which choice is *right*.

The programme will probably provide the kids with a number of "strategies" or "methodologies" to use when making moral choices, or when deciding what values to live their lives by. The first time you read one of these "methodologies" (some 5-step or 7-step system for choosing) you may not notice the subjectivism and relativism it teaches. This is because the HEB is not staffed by fools, but by highly-intelligent civil servants who know a thing or two about the use of language! They are most clever about phrasing their stuff so that the parent who has only a quick glance through the programme won't notice its operative philosophy.

But there is a simple trick you can use for testing these "methodologies" which I finally worked out for my own use. The handbook will tell the classroom Facilitator to teach the "methodology" by getting the kids to use it for solving some quite complex moral problem – one that would stymie the wisest of moral theologians until he got his bearings. Well, *forget* about using the "methodology" on *that* problem! That moral quandary was made up precisely so that the relativism and subjectivism inherent in the "methodology" *wouldn't* show up.

So forget that ambiguous quandary, and apply the "methodology" to some totally unambiguous moral choice: to some unequivocally-evil deed which some real or fictional person chose to do. Think about Macbeth, or Raskolnikov. Think about Hitler, or Lenin, or the Pol Pot regime in Cambodia. Think about any evil choice that comes to mind.

Then pretend *you* (not the character who did it, but *you*!) are trying to decide whether to do it or not. Apply the "methodology' the programme gives you. The result (which I pretty much guarantee) will astonish you. You will find that the "methodology" does *nothing whatever* to hinder you from choosing to do what the villain did. Nothing whatever! And it may, here and there, even *favour* that choice, in some subtle way.

How, you may wonder, do these Facilitators get away with providing such "methodologies"? If they really work that way, in practice? How come the trainees don't notice that the HEB programme teaches the art of making moral choices without reference to moral criteria?

Well, I *said* these Facilitators are clever; didn't I? The HEB pulls it off by two devices: first, by considering every subject in strictly psychological terms; and second, by using highly-deceptive pseudo-Christian language, which makes the thing seem, to an unwary reader, almost charitable. But it's an ersatz charity. It's bogus. It's counterfeit, and the falsity shows up when we apply the right touchstone.

For instance, when introducing its "Relationships" unit (page 69) the handbook does quite a lot to get the trainees to accept total relativism, but does it by using these techniques. It goes on about "responding" to others; about being "understanding" and about "generating trust" – and all that language sounds terribly, terribly *kind* and compassionate, so it comes across as vaguely Christian. And when the HEB says, piously, "We must respect the perceptions of others and accept the limitations of our own" that also sounds Christian. One almost gets the feeling the HEB is recommending a kind of humility!

But in that *same* introduction the handbook suggests constantly that there is no truth, and so no one can *ever* be objectively right or wrong about *anything*. Which is, of course, false. It's relativism; subjectivism. Yet the trainee might not notice those philosophical evils, in the midst of all that "caring" language. When the HEB says, for instance, that

> At any point in time, each person's perception of a given situation is valid for that person even if it differs from yours,

the trainee could easily miss the import of that statement. He could accept it without question, letting it slide into his mind as a "caring" sentiment. But it isn't; it's a lie. In fact, it's a *damned* lie – using the word "damned" in its full original sense.

Do you doubt me? Then try the test: ask yourself whether Adolf Hitler's "perception" of the Jewish "situation" around 1942 was "valid for him", just as, for instance, Blessed Titus Brandsma's "perception" of that same "situation" (for stating which perception he was martyred) was "valid for him". Or ask yourself whether you really want your kids to think that Stalin's "perception" of the "Gulag situation" was just as "valid for him" as Solzhenitsyn's was "for him"! Or for that matter, was Pontius Pilate's "perception" of the "Jesus situation" really "valid for him"? If we use that sort of test, we see right away what the programme is really teaching – in spite of the pseudo-piety in all that befuddling stuff about being "non-judgemental".

According to the HEB's philosophy of man, objective rational choice is impossible for human beings confronted with moral problems. Now, we all know such choice isn't *easy*! Hardly anything in this life is more difficult, and we very often fail to choose right. But still, it is possible for normal people to make morally-right choices, and we ought to aim at making such choices. In order to be capable of such choices a person needs to know something about logical thinking. He doesn't need to be a professor of logic, or have a head full of syllogisms – but he needs a habitual grasp of the basics, such as many of us were taught in our primary schools if we had good teachers and went to those schools before "facilitation" came in. He also needs certain virtues – prudence and fortitude mainly – and one acquires those through practice. He needs an objective standard of morality to judge things by, too: such as the Commandments. (And he needs Grace. But we can all have plenty of *that* – if we only ask for it.)

Thus equipped, the normal human being *can* make sound moral choices. Sometimes he'll need to puzzle over them, and sometimes he'll know right away that something is right or wrong. But it can be done. It's possible. Difficult, but possible! (If it were not possible, no person could ever be morally responsible for any of his acts, remember.)

The HEB does not agree. The HEB says right moral choices are impossible – because there is no objective moral standard by which choices can be judged, and no one able to perceive them if there were. Everybody's standard is "right for him", provided he's thought it over, is happy with it, has affirmed it and acted on it, etc. The HEB does not believe in "the standards of a normative rationality"; it believes neither in the rational mind, nor in objective norms.

So all things considered, this training programme amounts to a sustained attack on objective morality. It uses psychologically sophisticated techniques for introducing and reinforcing the habitual assumption that there is no truth, and the kindred assumption that even if there were, the human mind could not perceive it. Virtually all its exercises seem devised to get participants accustomed to regarding all value judgements as choices made on mere personal preference, with no grounding in objective reality whatsoever. Each person's choice – no matter what it is ! – is "true for him". Here is some more HEB prose on choice:

> A decision is based on *alternatives* . . . We tend to choose the alternative which offers the greatest amount of *positive reward*. The attractiveness of an alternative will depend on how we evaluate it. What one person considers worthwhile may have no rewarding characteristics for another (page 128).

No moral choice, for the HEB, can be based on objective truth or goodness perceived by the rational mind of the chooser. Here is how the HEB says we make our decisions:

> Decisions cannot be made as if they are problems in logic or just by looking at the pros and cons of the situation. Our choices are a combination of rational thinking, past experiences, personal needs and values, personality traits on the one hand, and pressures from without on the other (page 128).

Do you recall how down in Cork, the Facilitators' handbook explicitly abjured the idea that the rational mind is meant to *direct* human behaviour? The Ógra Chorcaí book calls rational self-direction "authoritarian" and outmoded; it insists that the mind should be permitted no authority over the person's acts. Instead, all of the person's faculties should remain, "democratically", on one level, with no precedence given to the reason.

The HEB holds much the same view: that the person's rational mind merely *participates* in decisions on an equal footing with a multiplicity of competing forces: a host of "past experiences"; a plethora of "personal needs and values"; a welter of "personality traits" and a battalion of "pressures from without".

Clearly, the HEB does not see the rational mind as meant to *direct* human choices according to those "standards of a normative rationality" Alasdair

40

MacIntyre wrote about! No; for the HEB, the intelligence is allowed only a subordinate, functionary role in the management of the person. Because the HEB does not recognise that any course of action *can* be objectively more right than any other (everyone's perception of reality is "true for him") the job of the reason is simply to accept whatever the person happens to find attractive, appealing, or likely to produce "positive rewards", and then to devise means by which the person might reach his desired goal as efficiently as possible. That is, the mind is there merely to act in an executive capacity; it is not meant to select the goals pursued.

That is my judgement of this HEB programme. In the next few chapters, I'll try to show how the thing actually works.

CHAPTER 5

Inducing Docility

The first unit in the HEB programme begins with an "ice-breaker" session. The trainees are told to mingle around being friendly. "Meet and greet as many members as you can," says the manual; "Try to remember first names." Then they have to choose "sharing" partners ("someone you don't know so well") and tell one another their reasons for being on the course. It's all surpassingly chummy – much chummier, in fact, than we would normally expect the first session of a professional training course, conducted by a state agency, to be.

Why is it so chummy? Well, my theory is that the chumminess is there to create an atmosphere which the HEB might describe as "trustful" or "co-operative", but which I – from my quite different perspective – would call "docile" and "obedient". That is, the HEB wants its trainees to accept its philosophy, and then go back to their schools and devise, introduce and "facilitate" programmes based on that philosophy. In other words, it wants docility: unquestioning acceptance.

But not all the teachers who take this course fully accept the HEB's philosophy when they enter the programme. The majority probably do, at this point – since the programme is given to teachers who volunteer. But even now, *all* are not sympathetic. So the HEB wants to get the trainees into an accepting frame of mind.

William Kirk Kilpatrick, in *The Emperor's New Clothes: The Naked Truth About the New Psychology* (Crossway Books, 1985; page 139) describes an "encounter" conducted by Carl Rogers, the "humanistic" psychologist most responsible for the theories behind these school "facilitation" programmes. At this gathering one teacher – whose attempts to "facilitate" were frustrated by a local school board member who disliked "facilitation" – asked Dr. Rogers what should be done about this recalcitrant and obstructive person. (That is, about a man who disagreed with him!) Dr. Rogers said,

> If we could get that school councillor into a three- or four-day encounter group, all kinds of things would change.

At this point, says Dr. Kilpatrick, there were

> murmurs of approval from others in the group . . . *If we could . . . he'd have to see the light then . . .*

Exactly what would happen to this benighted school board member once bundled off to a weekend encounter is left to the imagination. Presumably that rigid character armour would come unfastened.

And probably the disarming process would begin with some cosy "sharing"! It would end, Dr. Rogers clearly believed, with the man's willing surrender to the group's belief that "facilitation" is of help to the "facilitated".

But that surrender would not come about because the man had taken thought and decided that he had been objectively wrong in his judgements. No; he would surrender for strictly *psychological* reasons. He would surrender because the "encounter" process had somehow managed to merge him into the group; had weakened his ability to stand outside the pro-"facilitation" mentality and apply his own independent standards of judgement. Instead, he would be psychologically incorporated into the "encounter" group, and thus come to share its feelings and attitudes.

I suspect that Dr. Rogers' advice might well succeed. I don't think many of us would be able to resist that inbuilding process totally. We are weak, fallen creatures, after all! I fear that if I were put through the HEB's programme, the experience would damage my confidence in my own standards and judgement. A saint could resist it, of course – but I'm not a saint.

The first step in this psychological incorporation process is an engineered chumminess, an ersatz sociability (often augmented by pseudo-games) which makes the participant feel that he really isn't on a course of study but in something else. This is essential, because if we feel we are enrolled in a course of study, we normally try to *analyse ideas* which are put to us. We stand apart; we consider; we judge – and if we are not convinced, we argue our case. That is *normal* behaviour, in academic courses of study; in genuine seminars, etc. Such occasions are felt to *call for* the use of critical intelligence – normally.

But it is always difficult to use one's critical intelligence (or at least to express its conclusions) on social occasions. This is doubly true if the social occasion includes those who are our professional superiors, or who hold power over our jobs. For instance, if you were a guest at the wedding of your employer's daughter, what would you say if the mother of the bride expressed contempt for the Church to which you belong? Or for the rational mind? Or if she said she was *so* glad the young couple had gone to their local health board to get kitted out for contraception before the wedding?

Would you express your mind freely, as you might in some academic debate on such questions? Of *course* you wouldn't! Neither would I. We'd all feel that such remarks were out of place at that wedding. We'd think it was boorish – even almost immoral – to advert to truth or morality, or to praise God's gift of a rational mind, in such circumstances.

Well, the HEB programme puts the trainees in much the same position, right from the start. They know before they arrive that the HEB holds power over them professionally, of course. And then, on top of that, the HEB makes them behave as if the programme were some social gathering – which it *isn't*. Once the trainee starts behaving as if it were a gathering of friends (plus bosses) he's unlikely to disagree verbally with what is said. He might even start feeling as if it wasn't "nice" to disagree! That's what this initial fake chumminess does to promote docility. As the programme progresses, this feeling will be increased because the trainee will be incessantly told that everyone in the group must be "supportive", etc. By the end, unless the trainee has remarkable powers of resistance, he'll most likely have acquired the habit of stifling any critical thought that comes to mind during group sessions, as something unfit to speak: something out of place, inappropriate, unhelpful. If he's really drawn in, he'll even feel almost *guilty* about entertaining such thoughts.

That is, he may feel guilty about his *own ideas*. About what his own rational mind tells him. About what he himself perceives about reality. Clever – isn't it? This programme was not devised by amateurs. It is as sophisticated an instrument of intellectual corruption as our age has produced. Because it *is* intellectual corruption to diminish a rational being's inner freedom to use his own critical intelligence. But this programme corrupts the intellect by psychological means: it relies upon *feelings* created in artificially-engineered pseudo-social situations.

I call this first device – the trick of making the course seem like a social gathering in which the critical intelligence would be out of place – the "Polly-Put-the-Kettle-On" gimmick. Another device the HEB uses is one I call the "Of Course Everyone Knows" gimmick.

This gimmick consists in making the most outrageously contentious statements, as if those statements were not at all contentious, but platitudinous. As if of course *everyone* would instantly agree; of course there simply was no debate about it! This is extremely effective in producing docile acquiescence – or what looks very like it to all involved.

If you are in some group of people you don't know too well, and this group contains people you are eager, for professional reasons, to get on well with, how do you react if one of them says something like "Of course we all *know* the Pope is a Polish fascist" – and most people nod sagely?

Do you spill your tea laughing, and ask if they are having you on? Well, maybe – but maybe not. Just imagine yourself into that situation, and think about what you would probably do and say – if you had the feeling that you were the *only* person present who didn't regard it as a foregone conclusion that the Pope was a Polish fascist.

It's the "foregone conclusion" element that does it, I think. If you were in the same group, and someone said, "I read an article saying the Pope was a Polish fascist the other day. What do you people think?" then of course you would *easily* say the idea was absolute nonsense. If it were put that way, perhaps the whole group would chime in, agreeing with you.

44

The *idea* expressed was the same preposterous idea, in both cases. But in one case it would be easy to disagree, and in the other quite difficult – psychologically. Well, that is exactly the same gimmick the HEB employs throughout this programme. It presents any number of thoroughly false ideas and thoroughly reprehensible teaching techniques as acceptable ones. And when doing so it always *behaves* as if those ideas were ones all "aware" people will of course share, and as if those techniques were ones no normal person would object to. Of course. *Everybody* knows.

This gimmick also, I believe, dictates that the HEB Facilitators conducting this training course never suggest that school "facilitation" is itself a hotly-debated *moral* issue, not only in Ireland but across the western world. They *know* that their ideas and methods have been severely criticised on moral grounds, of course! I'm sure they are quite familiar with the addresses in which, for instance, Dr. McNamara, the Archbishop of Dublin, has criticised those ideas and methods. I'm sure they are well aware that in the USA parents were so outraged – on largely moral grounds – by these same ideas and methods that they lobbied the Congress to pass a law making it illegal for schools to use these methods on any child without his parents' prior written consent. Oh yes; they *know*. But they never allude to such facts; instead, they constantly suggest that all normal people think these ideas and methods excellent. If they are forced to acknowledge the existence of criticism, they ignore the fact that such criticism is widespread and based on moral grounds. They try to suggest that there is hardly any criticism, and that what little there is derives from some sort of mental derangement.

There is only one session in the entire training manual which in any way hints at the existence of resistance to these "facilitation" programmes. And that session, as you will discover later on, embodies that criticism in a mock debate between a neurotic old principal and an idealistic young teacher.

In training sessions so conducted, it would take an exceedingly brave and independent-minded trainee to question the moral acceptability of any idea or method put to him. A trainee who managed this feat would be rather like the fly which, caught in a spider's web, manages to move its wings so forcefully that the web itself is broken. It *can* happen – but it is rare! To do it in this course, a trainee would more or less have to interrupt the proceedings, stand up and say, "I think this entire programme is a cheat" – or words which, if politer in vocabulary, would in substance assert the same thing.

Such a trainee would have much in common with the Reluctant Cannibal, in the Flanders and Swann song of that name. Do you remember? He was a young man – son of the cannibal chief, as I recall – who refused all food at the feast. He stood up and declared, "Eating people is *wrong!*"

All the other cannibals present were shocked, exclaiming things like "What nonsense. Imagine saying eating people is wrong! Why, people have

45

always eaten people. If the Ju-Ju hadn't meant people to eat people, he wouldn't have made them of *meat*!"

The HEB Facilitators act just like those other cannibals. Except, unlike the cannibals, they actually know full well that the things they present as unquestionably acceptable are, in fact, being questioned all over the western world.

CHAPTER 6

Amateur Dramatics, Caringly Relating, and a Philosophical Goof: Still More Docility

The HEB's second unit is called "The Techniques of Group Discussion" – and here, the Facilitators' name for the kind of discussion they recommend is "Socratic". Honestly, if this infernal programme were not such a serious moral danger, we might read it for *laughs*! Take this "Socratic' business, now. I mean, *no* thinker in western intellectual history was ever more devoted to the rational pursuit of objective truth than Socrates. Socrates was an intellectual's intellectual. He revelled in abstract concepts. He delighted in exposing sophistries – especially of the emotivist kind, as in the *Gorgias*. Everyone who knows Plato knows that.

And yet, these HEB Facilitators apply the name "Socratic" to "sharing" sessions from which the standards of a normative rationality are rigidly *excluded*. To sessions in which the participants are urged to express nothing but *feelings*. To sessions in which the use of the rational mind to draw general conclusions is not *permitted*. The handbook *insists* on this, saying things like

> Encourage the use of "I" statements. Keep the group in the here and now. Discourage generalisations and intellectualising.

That direction is found on page 28 – in the section introducing the technique of "Socratic" group discussion. *Gosh.*

This entire unit is devoted to substituting the habit of subjectivistic feeling-exchange for the habit of rational discussion and debate in pursuit of objective truth. Always the trainees are made to focus upon themselves, their personalities and their subjective feelings, rather than on any impersonal, objective truth or principle. On pages 35-36, for instance, the trainees are made to discuss their own "group skills". First, each one fills out a questionnaire on which he must grade himself on such matters as "Willingness to discuss personal feelings" (here the end-terms are "reticent" and "free"); "Likely to trust others" ("distrust" and "trust") and "Willingness to be influenced by others" ("resistant" and "flexible").

Anyone who does this questionnaire will quickly realise that the kind of person the HEB likes will score lots of points, because all the "nice" words (the words suggesting approbation) fall at the 10-point end of the scale, while the opposite words fall at the 1-point end. We find words like

47

"sensitive", "creative acceptance", "aware" and "free" at the upper end, and words like "resistant", "defensive", "unaware" and "insensitive" at the lower.

Trainees filling out this form (and then, of course, "sharing" what they presumably learn about themselves) cannot fail to see that if they want to be seen to possess "group skills", they will behave in an "accepting", "flexible", and "trusting" way throughout the course. That is, they won't disagree with what the Facilitator says: they'll be "accepting"! If the Facilitator, or the group (led by the Facilitator) arrives at one conclusion, but their own rational minds tell them this conclusion is false, they'll disregard their own minds and go with the group – because that's being "flexible", rather than "defensive". If an exercise asks them to reveal their personal feelings, they'll reveal them – to show how "free" they are. That's what they'll do, if they swallow this stuff about "group skills".

But if we translate those terms into *our* language (normal English) we'll see that the qualities which are discouraged here are independence of mind, confidence in one's own ability to think, rationality, critical intelligence, etc. Precisely the *Socratic* qualities – if we use the word "Socratic" in its dictionary meaning of "like Socrates".

Throughout this programme, the HEB teaches its trainees to be as unlike Socrates as possible – by means of what it calls "Socratic" discussions. Which reminds me of the old joke about the man who was feeling terribly woebegone and was told by a friend, "Take my advice. Be *philosophical*. Don't think about it!"

These HEB people are extremely clever with language, as I keep saying. They are clever in the same way a capable advertising man, or PR expert, is clever with words; the way those sophists Socrates takes on in the *Gorgias* were clever with words. Let's look at one of the word-pairs in this "group skills" quiz: "reticent" and "free". Isn't it quite ludicrous that people should be led to behave so subserviently as to reveal their personal feelings to virtual strangers in a classroom – simply because some Facilitator *tells* them to! – in order to show that they are "free"? It's sheer Newspeak, this "Facilitationese" – isn't it?

Myself, I do not see such subservience as a sign of freedom. I think it's a sign of loss of freedom. The loss of freedom that goes with loss of backbone. It takes a bit of backbone to protect one's privacy by exercising a rational reticence when one is pressured to abandon that reticence. The spineless are *not* free people, internally. And they seldom remain free externally for long. Protecting one's freedom in the real world calls for precisely the qualities this exercise, and the rest of this pernicious programme, seem created to destroy.

This destruction process works by constantly forcing the trainees to focus their attention upon themselves – to get them wondering if their own personalities are up to snuff, psychologically. Wondering if they are normal –

48

as the "humanistic" psychologist understands normality. Constantly the HEB suggests to them, in one way after another, that the trainee who resists merging himself into the group so as to share its ("facilitated") emotions and attitudes, is psychologically inadequate. He lacks "understanding". He is "insensitive" and "unaware". He doesn't "know how to listen".

Which, translated into normal English, means he possesses independence of mind, he values objectivity, and he has the courage to withstand group pressure! In other words, he isn't a *pushover*. He's still free.

AMATEUR DRAMATICS

The third unit is called "Role Playing". In its introduction to this unit the HEB expresses wholehearted enthusiasm for this psychotherapeutic technique – and in doing so, speaks with amazing frankness about its reason for holding this technique in such high esteem. For instance, on page 51 it says:

> The technique of role play is probably one of the most powerful available for promoting behaviour change.

Such statements, about this or that psychological technique, recur throughout the programme. Here is another statement (page 10) also asserting the HEB's belief that "health educators" should manipulate the kids by working on their emotions so as make them behave as the HEB desires:

> There is a growing awareness that the traditional cognitive model of teaching is not effective in health education . . . The affective component must be introduced with the intention of bringing about behaviour modification.

The HEB prefers to use the word "affective" instead of "emotional". It means the same thing, however! Just check your dictionary. Here's another frankly emotivist statement, from page 5:

> . . . the process of health education . . . aims at shifting the knowledge of health subjects from theory to action . . . Therefore, it is necessary to learn ways and means of presenting knowledge about health subjects that will bring about an affect (sic) on people's behaviour. Teaching health must move further than the cognitive domain and concern itself with affective learning.

All those are quintessentially *emotivist* statements. In saying the above, the HEB was shamelessly asserting that it seeks to manipulate others emotionally by the use of psychological devices. If you don't quite see what I mean, look back to the definition of emotivism I took from Alasdair MacIntyre, in the first chapter of this book.

"Role play" is a variant of the psychotherapeutic technique called "psycho-drama" which was developed for use in group therapy. When this technique is used in mental hospitals the psychiatrist conducting the treatment starts by giving the patients a resumé of some life situation which recalls the past life of one or more members of the group. Then the patients – including those whose actual lives are involved – do some "role playing". That is, they improvise dramatically within the various parts. They say what they feel those people might say; they express the feelings which arise in them during the drama.

These situations usually involve conflict; most often, family or marital conflict. As the "role play" proceeds, the psychiatrist hopes they will express more and more of their *own* feelings, which he and the group will then discuss.

One does not have to be a psychiatrist to see that such techniques, which may be helpful if used in controlled situations in mental institutions, could be exceedingly dangerous under different conditions, and in the wrong hands. Obviously such techniques could easily be used by the unscrupulous for ideological or even personal ends. Equally obviously, if such techniques are used within the general community, whatever is said about others in the sessions could easily become part of community gossip – even if totally untrue. After all, the other parties to the conflicts are not present to put *their* side of these stories – are they?

Yet this same technique is now used all over Ireland, with HEB-trained teachers doing the psychiatrist's job. In these sessions, the kids are asked to act out the conflicts they have with their parents – and of course the parents are never invited in to put their side of things. (Usually the parents are not even aware that this is going on in school. The manual containing the North Western Health Board's "Lifeskills" programme actually tells the teachers to get a "contract" from each class group, at the start of each school year. This "contract" involves a promise, on the part of the kids, not to tell what goes on in the class. Which is another reason why parents don't know this is going on.)

But those dangers are not my only objection to "role play" as a form of "facilitation". Apart from the danger of spreading calumny, and of doing the sort of harm always possible whenever people practice medicine without medical expertise, this "role play" functions as a tool for "facilitating" others into accepting the attitudes, ideas and emotions the Facilitators want them to accept. That is, as a tool for emotivist manipulation.

Within this teacher-training programme, "role-play" is used on the trainees in order to foster attitudes of scorn and contempt for those who do not think "facilitation" programmes are good for children. The trainees

50

are put through "role play" exercises meant to teach them how to cope with those of us who protest against these programmes. With, that is, such people as parents, principals, other teachers, school governors, parish priests, bishops, and journalists who write anti-"facilitation" books like the one you are reading! In this unit (on pages 58-59) we find a "role play" of this type, involving two characters. The one who is against "facilitation" is a crusty old principal who doesn't like newfangled ideas and who wants kids' noses to be held firmly to the grindstone all day long. He is also neurotically afraid of losing "control" over the kids and the school. *Those* are his objections to "facilitation" programmes; he has no *moral* objections whatsoever, and he is an autocrat who does not respect human freedom. And yet this "role play" session is the *only* place in the manual where the HEB recognises the existence of objections to "facilitation" programmes!

The other character is a noble young teacher, well-trained in "health education" – or "pastoral care"; this paragon prefers this pious-sounding term, but it means "facilitation" all the same. He is devoutly eager to help the children.

Reading the scenario in the handbook, I couldn't help wondering how the trainees manage to keep themselves from laughing aloud at these characterisations. I mean, the thing is so obvious; so crude. Here is what the person who is to play Crusty Old Principal is told, in order to understand his role:

> You know that pastoral care is a way of providing students with soft options. You pointed this out at the last staff meeting. Yet, this young man/woman is seeking a meeting with you to put forward his/her proposals. You have put him/her off twice and you have now decided to see him/her and make him/her understand that while he/she means well, he/she is far too inexperienced and his/her ideas are *not acceptable* in your school.

Funny, isn't it? Like some heavy husband or father in a Victorian melodrama. Who would take such a characterisation of us anti-"facilitation" people seriously? In contrast, here is a bit of what the person playing Noble Young Teacher is given, to prepare for his role:

> You have undertaken in-service training in groupwork and pastoral care at your own expense . . . You are determined to fight for a caring service for students in this school . . . The students are depending on you. You won't let them down.

The handbook also gives Noble Young Teacher the arguments he is to use against Crusty Old Principal:

51

You . . . are convinced that the system is far too autocratic. You also feel that there is too much emphasis on cognitive learning and exam results to the neglect of other aspects of the students' development. You believe that the students should have a far greater involvement in their own learning and be provided with opportunities for decision-making. After all, young people today have to go out into a world where they are confronted with decisions on every side. Yet, in your opinion, they have to go through a system which has a "sit down, shut up, and speak when you are spoken to" philosophy.

All right. You have read my arguments against "facilitation" up to now. Does *that* argument meet *mine* in any way at all? Of course not! Noble Young Teacher is in conflict with Crusty Old Principal, not with people like myself who object to "facilitation" on moral grounds. And as for that stuff about autocracy, well, is it any less autocratic to manipulate kids through their emotions (by using psycho-therapeutic techniques) into doing what you want them to do? Is that really less abusive of their freedom than Crusty Old Principal's autocratic ways? But those of us who criticise "facilitation" detest it precisely *because* it violates the teenager's human freedom - which is a *rational* freedom - by trying to manipulate him through his emotions.

Yet when the HEB trains teachers to reply to us, it sets up Crusty Old Principal to represent all who oppose "facilitation". Now, I have had some experience of conflict with Facilitators. So have many parents! And we find that they will often respond to our clear *moral* criticisms, or our attempts to show how these programmes deny the kids their rational *freedom*, by saying exactly the sort of thing Noble Young Teacher is here taught to say. When this happens, I get a rather eerie feeling - as if I had said, "The daffodils are past their best", and someone replied, "How dare you say there is a purple cow in the garden!"

But then, inventing a straw man and demolishing his arguments (rather than the actual arguments of your real opponent in debate) is a very old rhetorical device, so it's really no surprise to meet it here - or in the many puff-pieces journalists now write in the secularist press touting these programmes. But I think this "role play" session involves more than the unscrupulous debater's trick. I think it also employs a subtle psychological mechanism to harden the hearts of the trainees against us anti-"facilitation" people.

I said earlier that the characterisation of Crusty Old Principal is so crude it is almost comic. Now, those who wrote this thing are not stupid people. They know the effect of words, with which they can be quite diabolically clever. So I suspect they know perfectly well that this characterisation is comic. I think they must expect at least some of the trainees to play the part for laughs.

As the role is written, it would be very difficult not to do that. Once the player got going, it would be almost inevitable that he start exaggerating the neurotically-hidebound quality of Crusty Old Principal. The role-player would find it hard not to let COP contradict himself, or get enraged to the point of spluttering incoherently, or otherwise make himself ridiculous. The role, as written, all but demands such treatment.

Which would have an interesting psychological effect on all present. There would be general hilarity, into which the trainees would all be drawn. That is, they would be drawn into a kind of *complicity*. Now, the person who finds himself in a group which has begun to laugh cruelly at a caricature of real but absent people, must either confront the general mood in an outspoken way, or become part of it. There is no middle course at such times because if we do not find the courage to oppose the mood, we always find it much harder to stand out against the attitudes and assumptions which caused it later on. In this instance, the cruel and dishonest caricature is of an anti-"facilitation" person. At other times and places, the cruel and dishonest caricatures have been of Jews or "natives" or "bourgeois running dogs". But the psychological effect is the same.

As I keep saying, this programme was not written by amateurs.

CARINGLY RELATING

The next unit is called "Relationships". But here the HEB does not have sexual or family relations primarily in mind – because this programme is meant to train Facilitators, not to work directly upon the young. So this unit concentrates on developing the habit of subjectivism in the trainees. What the unit does is give them still further practice in thinking and speaking in purely subjective terms, no matter what the actual subject under discussion might be.

They are given several more personality questionnaires to fill out and then "share". Every exercise in the unit is about the personalities and emotions of the trainees themselves. And when discussing these already-subjective matters, they are led always to speak in subjective terms, to "express feelings".

For instance, the manual advises the trainees against telling a person that his ideas are untrue. Instead it advises them to use language which "is descriptive rather than evaluative" (page 71). And true to form, they bedeck this emotivist advice to eschew rational judgement with "caring" talk about "feelings": with language which sounds almost Christian – in a psychological sort of way:

> Describing one's own reaction leaves the other individual free to use it or not as he sees fit. Avoiding evaluative language reduces the need for

the other individual to react defensively.

When we *think* about that advice, of course, it soon becomes clear that it is simply untrue. In fact, it is the *opposite* of the truth, because the fact is that when two people discussing an issue stick firmly to the objective question itself, and just talk about what might be *true* about that question, they are unlikely to feel any need to "react defensively". If a person says to me, "I think your ideas about the HEB are not true", there's nothing remotely *personal* in what he says – so of course I don't feel the slightest desire to get cross with him. Why should I? People disagree about *issues* all the time. Like any other normal adult, I'm quite used to intellectual differences of opinion. Aren't you?

However, if such a person were to follow the HEB's advice, and say "Your book made me feel terribly unhappy. I found it a *hurtful* book!" then how might I respond? I might feel rather cross at being told that I was being "hurtful". I might resent the implication that I was a bully. Mightn't you?

But these HEB Facilitators, because they do not believe in an objective moral order; because they do not believe in truth itself, or the mind's ability to know it; naturally cannot conceive of a two people disagreeing *intellectually*. They see all disagreements as emotional conflicts, because they are emotivists who think all value judgements are *nothing but* expressions of feeling or of culturally-conditioned attitudes.

CHAPTER 7

Systematising Screwtape:
"Values Clarification"

The next unit is about "values clarification" – and this is a subject which really deserves a book all to itself. It is impossible to do justice to the adroit *sneakiness* of this method of inculcating subjectivism and moral relativism in the few pages available here.

However, one must *try* – so I'll begin by noting that the name "values clarification" – like everything else about the technique! – is deceptive. Most people – parents, teachers, priests, school principals, bishops – upon first hearing of an educational method known as "values clarification", will naturally suppose that the method has something to do with clarifying young people's thinking, so that they will become more capable of perceiving objectively *true* values. Isn't that what you would suppose, if you heard the term for the first time? It's certainly what I would innocently assume – if I hadn't actually read some books containing these exercises.

In making that innocent assumption I would be wrong, however. Dead wrong! "Values clarification" has *nothing whatever* to do with the recognition of objectively true values. Those who invented it do not believe that objective truth exists. They are total moral and philosophical relativists; they are subjectivists and emotivists. And usually (outside of Ireland) they are quite frank about saying so.

The men most responsible for this technique are an American educator and secular humanist called Sidney Simon, and his colleagues in the "humanistic education movement". In an essay called "Values" (found in *Readings in Values Clarification*, ed. by Sidney Simon and Howard Kirschenbaum: Winston, 1973) Dr. Simon and his close colleague Merrill Harmin say that the approaches to values they think best

> are not based upon the assumption that absolute goods exist and can be known. They view values as relative, personal, and situational. The main task of these approaches is not to identify and transmit the "right" values, but to help a student to clarify his own values so that he can obtain the values that best suit him and his environment . . .

The same collection of essays contains a piece by Farnum Gray called "Doing Something About Values". Mr. Gray is an *aficionado* of "values clarification", and his essay is an adulatory account of an "encounter" for educationists conducted by Dr. Simon. Here is Mr. Gray's description of Dr. Simon's talk, while in a relatively unbuttoned state just after a good lunch:

Simon sprawls shirtless in the New England sun at the lunch break and discusses the subject . . . "There has to be an absence of a right-answer syndrome . . . Put the focus on process, search, inquiry" . . . He warns that teachers must be alert to keep "moralising crap" out of their work with values.

For Dr. Simon and his ilk, education in values has nothing whatever to do with truth; with teaching kids about an objective moral order in which some things actually *are* right and good and other things are not, regardless of how we may *feel* about it. Dr. Simon is a relativist who believes that words like "true" and "good" have only a subjective meaning, which varies from person to person. He takes as his own the sentiment Hamlet expressed, feigning madness: "There's nothing either good or bad, but thinking makes it so". He believes we must *create* our own values or, if we adopt those of others, we must do so simply because we find they "suit" us; they accord well with our chosen "self-image". For Dr. Simon, the teacher who tries to show that some form of behaviour is *objectively* right or wrong is simply spouting "moralising crap". The HEB, in its introduction (on pages 90-92) to this unit on "values clarification", speaks in the same terms:

> As health educators . . . we must resist the tendency to "tell" and to "teach". We must . . . avoid the danger of imposing our values on others. Our aim should be to help the individual to become self-directed, autonomous and responsible in the complex world of today . . . value clarification . . . avoids attempting to teach values and encourages the individual to discover his own values – the values he lives by.

Thus the HEB does not define a value as a *truth* upon which a person might base his life; the HEB studiously avoids language which might suggest that objective truth exists. Instead, it defines "value" as

> an enduring belief upon which we act by preference or a learned conception of what is desirable. Put simply, a value is a guide or norm or principle by which we live. It is made up of beliefs and/or attitudes which tend to make us behave in a particular way.

Like everyone else, the HEB knows that children acquire values from parents, Church, friends, books, etc. But the HEB does not recognise that this acquisition may involve the *recognition* of some truth. For the HEB, the child is simply a creature being conditioned, rather than a human being who can, in a simple way at first, perceive reality. The HEB pictures the child taking in values by pleasant associations, just as Pavlov's dogs came

56

to associate the pleasurable sensations of eating with the sound of the bell which announced their meals. Here is a bit of HEB prose on this:

> The child chooses what he feels is important, familiar, perhaps associated with a family member or pleasant activity . . . Memory of a special day of swimming or climbing or learning to ride a bicycle, will establish "exercise" as fun . . .

Then, says the HEB, comes adolescence, when these conditioned values must be tested, and the ones which no longer "suit" the individual discarded.

Now of course it is true that during adolescence we normally sift the values, ideas, etc. we have been taught. We often discard some of our parents' values too: parents *can* be wrong, and if they are found wrong about something (when their ideas are judged by an *objective* standard as best we can) then of course we must depart from those ideas. No sensible person would deny that.

But if we are doing this as befits rational human beings, we do this sifting on the basis of *truth*. We do not simply say to ourselves, "I now find this value unattractive; it doesn't suit my personality or self-concept, so I'll throw it in the dustbin. It's just not my *style*!"

Yet that is exactly what the HEB recommends. The HEB would teach young people simply to work out what values they find comfortable and attractive as a matter of mere personal preference or taste, and then "affirm" and act upon those values. Like choosing a new dress or tie.

And *why* does the HEB say the teenager normally looks over his acquired values, to see which now *suit* him, and which he no longer *likes*? According to the HEB, this process starts when we find that certain values we have been taught are *demanding*: that they pose "difficulty" for us!

> When a child enters adolescence and young adulthood, he begins to question the values he adopted from others and their primary sources. He starts to make choices about what values he wishes to retain and what ones he now finds difficulty in retaining.

The basic method of "values clarification" consists in applying certain rules of thumb to this sorting-out process – in order to discover which values we "wish to retain", because they *suit* our personalities. The HEB teaches the seven-step process for this choice of values which was originally invented by Sidney Simon and his colleagues. Here is the way Dr. Simon expresses these seven steps, in *Meeting Yourself Halfway: 31 Value-Clarification Strategies for Daily Living* (Argus, 1974):

Before something can be a full value, it must meet these criteria. It

must be:
1. chosen freely
2. chosen from among alternatives
3. chosen after due reflection
4. prized and cherished
5. publicly affirmed
6. acted upon
7. part of a pattern that is a repeated action.

We have only to reflect upon those seven criteria for a moment to realise that they do nothing whatever to sort out good and true values from bad and false ones. Any of the great, single-minded villains of history could easily apply those criteria to the values upon which he acted, and come up full of cheerful "self-acceptance" as a result. Adolf Hitler, for example, could apply those criteria to his values – such as "Aryan supremacy". He could ask, "Have I chosen this value freely, or was it forced on me by someone else? Some parent or teacher?" And obviously, his choice was free and his own: he actually made that value up. Did he choose it from alternatives? Of course he did; he had non-racist values available to him, like every other Catholic schoolboy of his generation! Did he reflect duly? Yes, indeed; he even wrote a long book containing those reflections. Did he prize and cherish his value? Why, yes; it would not be exaggeration to say that he cherished that value, and his others, to the point of death. He was nothing if not *faithful* to his self-chosen values, was Hitler! Did he affirm it publicly? Yes; countless times, in his book and in any number of speeches. Did he act upon it? Repeatedly? Yes, European Jewry was all but wiped out because he acted upon that "value" so many times. The Poles, Gypsies, and other "non-Aryans" had their numbers reduced by that repetition too.

But then, according to the technique taught by the HEB for sorting out the values we want to keep, Hitler's value comes out just *fine*. All his values meet the test admirably.

Well, yes! That is exactly what I've been saying, about "values clarification". It has nothing whatever to do with truth and goodness. All it does is give the individual some questions by which he may discover whatever values seem to be inside him; how much he personally *likes* those values, etc. That's all. And Hitler liked *his*.

The HEB wants Irish teenagers to apply these same seven criteria to the values they have been taught by home and Church. Especially, of course, to the ones the teenager "now finds difficulty in retaining"! What will happen when a teenager does so?

Well, let's find out. Let's apply those seven criteria to two values commanded by God, which Irish teenagers may well have been taught by home and/or Church: to honouring parents, and to chastity. Those *are* values most of us find considerable "difficulty in retaining", especially during adolescence – aren't they? How will they fare, by these seven criteria?

Not too well, for most of us. First of all, did we really choose those values freely, or were they taught to us by others? What do you think? Myself, I think that while some kids might be spontaneously inclined to honour their parents out of natural affection, others might not. And as for chastity, well, in a fallen world I think that one *has* to be taught. Few of us would think it up for ourselves!

How about the next one: choosing from alternatives? When most of us were taught those values, were we given a free choice about them? Or did our parents lay down the law a bit – especially about honouring them? Were we left free to be as rude as we pleased to them? Hardly! So once again, we have to answer No.

What about the third? The HEB, giving its gloss on this criterion, asks if the chooser gave "thoughtful consideration to each alternative". Well, I think we might just allow a tentative Yes on this question. I mean, many of us gave considerable consideration to the idea of telling our parents where to get off, quite often. Didn't we? As for chastity, many if not most adolescents consider the problem endlessly – but I'm not too sure that "thoughtful" is the right word for the consideration involved! Still, we might give this one a Yes. So that makes one Yes so far, out of three questions.

The next is a real doozy, I think. The HEB gloss fills out "prized and cherished", saying it means "cherishing, being happy with the choice". But really, how many kids are *happy* about either honouring their parents, or about chastity, during adolescence? Adolescence is almost *definable* as that time of life when both those values are irksome in the extreme. Isn't it? So we have to say No again. That makes one Yes, four Noes.

Next comes "affirming", which the HEB expands as being "willing to stand up publicly for the values we believe in". Goodness gracious me! How many of us, at 15 or so, were willing to stand up publicly and say we believed in honouring parents, or in being chaste? Wouldn't you have felt like a terrible goody-goody doing that? It depends a bit, I suppose, on who would be listening to your public affirmation. But how many teenage peer groups today (or even in our day!) would have been receptive to such public affirmations? Not too many, I think. And how many teenagers could honestly say they would be willing to make those affirmations, if those affirmations were sure to be greeted with jeers and hoots? So once more, I think the answer has to be No, for most people. That makes five Noes, one Yes.

And then we reach the two most difficult questions of all: the ones about how well the person customarily acts upon the value: about how well he actually lives up to it. About these questions, the HEB says:

The way we behave reveals our values . . . Values that we prize tend to be acted upon repeatedly. A pattern develops.

So what does the poor kid say, if he knows he hardly ever *really* lives up to those values? If he knows he cheeks his parents a good bit of the time? If his actual behaviour is not consistently chaste? Note, please, that the questions do not allow the teenager to say that when he behaves unchastely he is sorry afterwards! For the HEB, such sorrow is irrelevant; for the HEB, only actual behaviour reveals values.

God, of course, is more merciful: "Whose sins you shall forgive, they are forgiven." But the totalitarian mentality, unlike the Divine Mercy, is not interested in values people might hold, even though they find difficulty in living up to them. The totalitarian mind is interested only in results.

So what does the poor kid say – if his intentions are good, but his behaviour is frequently bad? He has to say No again. He has to say it twice, for questions six and seven: No; No. That makes one Yes, and six Noes.

And this, according to the "values clarification" experts in the HEB and elsewhere, means he *doesn't have* those two values! Apparently, they don't *suit* him. They are not "true for him".

That's how "values clarification" works, if we apply its criteria to two of the more demanding values taught by most Irish homes, and by the Church. Funny, isn't it? That the same criteria by which Adolf Hitler's value came up smiling, should prove so fatal to two values commanded by God?

So, if the teenager really takes his "values clarification" lessons seriously, he'll toss out "Honour thy father and thy mother" along with the sixth and ninth Commandments. He'll adopt some spiffing *new* values instead – ones which he might find less "difficulty in retaining". Such as, I suppose, "personal autonomy within the family" and "sexual freedom"? Then he could follow the HEB's directions about his new, self-chosen values:

> Participants should also be encouraged to "act" on their values, since this "acting" is an important element in a full value.

Thus, says the HEB, the young person will "clarify and work out a value system that will give him a sense of identity in today's world". Thus he will become "self-directed, autonomous and responsible in the complex world of today". These techniques, says the HEB, can help the young person

> to become more thoroughly aware of himself and consequently live in clear harmony with his beliefs.

The whole thing, of course, is *perverse*. The HEB, Sidney Simon and the rest of these "values clarification" people have got the whole business *backwards*. They say we should look inside ourselves and discover which of the values we were taught we are *already* acting upon consistently; which values we *feel* comfortable with, etc. Then, we should give up all attempts to live by values which we, because we are fallen, "find difficulty in retaining".

Our media are always saying that those who profess to hold values which they fail to live up to are hypocrites. The HEB does not use the word "hypocrisy" in the training manual, but clearly thinks along the same lines. But *is* it hypocrisy to hold values which we cannot, in all honesty, claim to be living up to consistently? If so, we are *all* hypocrites, if we do those things which we ought not to have done, and leave undone those things which we ought to have done. Which means, St. Paul was also a hypocrite, when he wrote

> My own actions bewilder me; what I do is not what I wish to do, but something which I hate . . . praiseworthy intentions are always ready to hand, but I cannot find my way to the performance of them; it is not the good my will prefers, but the evil my will disapproves, that I find myself doing . . . Pitiable creature that I am, who is to set me free from a nature thus doomed to death? Thanks be to God through Jesus Christ Our Lord!

Those who devised this programme are not amateurs, as I said earlier. The entire programme reads as if designed to *stop* people thinking in terms of objective goodness and truth; to keep people from thinking about what they ought to do, what they ought to value, if they would value that which is objectively true and good. "Values clarification" would, I think, appeal strongly to C. S. Lewis' wily old devil, Screwtape. Advising young Wormwood, a trainee devil, Screwtape said that when out on temptation duty a clever devil will do everything possible to fuddle his "patient"; that is, to keep him from thinking in terms of objective truth:

> The great thing is to make him value an opinion for some quality other than truth, thus introducing an element of dishonesty and make-believe into the heart of what otherwise threatens to become a virtue.

Those who invented "values clarification" have taken that instruction to heart, and systematised it into a pseudo-science. And then, they managed to pull off the cleverest stunt of all: they managed to persuade Christian educators that this "science" of theirs was the best method available for inculcating Christian values. Yes; they *did*. I'll try to explain how in the chapter after next. Wait for it.

CHAPTER 8

Moral Choice by Amoral Standards: The HEB on "Decision-Making"

The next chapter is about making choices. Here, the HEB teaches its trainees a five-step "goal-directed model" of choice, which "model" it expects those trainees, in their turn, to teach to your children.

But the HEB, with its philosophy, does not acknowledge that *moral* choices must be made by *moral* criteria. So it teaches a "model" of decision-making which omits such criteria entirely. This "model" asks the chooser to consider all sorts of things when making his (moral) choice – *except* which choice is objectively right and which choice is objectively wrong.

The HEB teaches that this "model" is to be used for *all* a person's choices – every one of them. It is meant to be used not merely for practical choices (such as, "Should I go to Cork by bus or train?") but for moral ones as well (such as, "Should I kill my sister?"). To the HEB, all choice is one, because there are no objective moral criteria to apply. Thus the HEB tells us (page 128) that "decision-making is the process of choices between alternative courses of action", and then goes on to give five examples of "choices" ranging from "whether to give up smoking" or "whether to tell the truth or a lie".

All those choices, the HEB teaches, are to be made by the same method, as if there was nothing different about those choices. As if all our choices were mere practical choices – like deciding whether to take the bus or the train. In making this assumption, the HEB is of course wrong (surpassingly wrong; unbelievably wrong; exotically wrong!) about the difference between moral questions and mere practical questions.

The HEB is also surpassingly wrong about the *real* reason why moral choice is such a problem for us poor mortals. The HEB goes on as if moral choice was a problem because most moral choices are inherently very complex. This is *not* so, in my experience; has it been true in yours? Yes, *some* of the moral choices I've made in my time were complex ones. But *most* were anything but! Most of my moral choices would have been simplicity itself for me – if I had not been under severe temptation when making them.

Think back over your past life, paying particular attention to your false moral choices. If your experience tallies with mine, then you made most wrong choices not because the ethical problem was really terribly complex, but simply because you wanted to. You were strongly tempted, and you fell. At least, that is the way it has been with me.

Most of the times I chose to do the wrong thing (and I've done that plenty of times!) I did so not because I was sincerely puzzled about what was right and what was wrong, but because the wrong choice strongly appealed to me, and I was too weak to resist the temptation. I lacked the requisite virtue. Usually, I lacked the courage and the humility to do what I really knew was right, rather than what was fashionable.

In that state, I sometimes agonised over my choices, in a way! I went through longish "song-and-dance routines" in which I tried (never quite successfully) to convince myself that the problem really *was* terribly complex; that there was no simple answer; that what I wanted to do really wasn't all *that* wrong at all. That is, I rationalised my choice. But almost always, at the bottom of my mind I was aware of what I was doing, and why.

Another way of putting this is to say that when I made those wrong choices, I was in a state of acute temptation. Why? Because I am a fallen creature, and the devil is good at his job! He *is* an angelic intelligence, you know. But nowhere in the HEB handbook will you find words like "temptation", "fallen", or even "creature". The HEB writes as if this were a prelapsarian world, inhabited by beings who more or less made themselves.

So now, when I examine the HEB's five-step method of decision-making, I'm going to put it to the sort of test it might meet in the *real* world. In a fallen world that is – not a prelapsarian one. In a world in which people are tempted to do wrong things. I'm going to use as my example the choice faced by a 15-year-old pregnant schoolgirl – a girl who is strongly tempted to have an abortion.

Is this asking too much of the five-step "model"? Is it putting too much strain on it? Of course not! The "model" is *meant* for moral choices, says the HEB. And when we test anything to see how much strain it will take, we test it by submitting it to the maximum strain it may have to face. We don't test a bridge, meant to support a 20-ton lorry, by driving a Morris Minor across it – do we? No. We build it strong enough to carry 20 tons, and then we apply 20 tons to it. That's just being realistic.

So that's our situation. Our test-case is a teenage girl, pregnant, who does *not* want to have a baby. Who is scared green of what her parents will say when they find out she's been fornicating. Who doesn't want to have to leave school. Who doesn't want her friends to know she's been "caught". Who just wants the whole horrible problem to *go away*.

This girl is going to apply the same five-step method of "decision-making" she learned from her "health" teacher in that convent school she doesn't want to leave. Why do I say it's a *convent* school? Because it probably is, that's why!

The HEB's first step (page 129) in its "goal-directed model" of decision-making reads as follows:

Step One: Outline/Define the Problem
        Do you understand the situation?
        Have you gathered all the facts?
        Have you a general idea of the outcome you want?

Here we see that at the outset (at the most crucial time, that is) the HEB does not suggest that moral considerations might be relevant to the present choice. It assumes that moral considerations are irrelevant, and asks the chooser *only* about knowledge, facts, and what outcome she *wants*.

She's very clear about what she *wants*! She wants not to be pregnant any more, so she can get on with her life as if it had never happened. That's why she's tempted. If I were a 15-year-old in her position, none of *those* questions would bring right and wrong to my mind. Step two (page 129) reads like this:

Step Two: Identify Alternatives:
        Have you found as many alternatives as you can?
        What did you do in similar situations in the past?
        What would others do in your position?
        Who can you turn to for advice on alternatives?
        Information – where can you get it?

Again, moral considerations do not appear. And not only that, but these questions subtly suggest that she really ought to consider *both* options. The HEB positively enjoins her to find "as many alternatives" as she can, and then consider them all *seriously*! This step uses the words "alternatives" *three* times. It tells her to get "advice" on these "alternatives". Which obviously calls to mind the various bodies which will advise her – *all* of them. That is, it calls to mind Cura and LIFE – but it also calls to mind the Well Woman Centre and its ilk. Does it give the edge to either type of adviser?

Yes; I think it does – subtly. It asks her where she can turn for advice on "alternatives". Doesn't that suggest to you that she is meant to find some adviser who claims to offer *all* the "alternatives" dispassionately? I think so. But only *one* kind of "adviser" claims *that*! Cura and LIFE make no such claim; they do not regard the decision as morally neutral.

Ruth Riddick, writing in *Rights* (the publication of the Irish Council for Civil Liberties – the issue is undated) said that the Well Woman Centre and Open Line Counselling

    offer a non-directive pregnancy counselling service, defined as offering women the opportunity of exploring the issues and implications of an unwanted pregnancy in a neutral environment. All the options will be discussed and the need for the client herself to determine which option is most appropriate for her will be stressed. Once the decision has been made, the counsellor will offer further practical assistance, as requested.

Note the word "appropriate" here. Like the HEB, Ms. Riddick does not speak in terms of right and wrong. Clients in her service will not be encouraged to think in moral terms, but in terms of what is "appropriate" for them. That is, in subjectivistic terms. The atmosphere will be "neutral", she says. That is, morally relativistic. A matter of personal preference.

So these questions suggest, in a subtle sort of way, that the Really Grown Up Thing To Do is find out all the choices, lay them out calmly, and decide which choice will best meet her individual "goals". If you were Screwtape, wouldn't you smile at all that?

If you were Screwtape, I think you'd also smile a bit at the one about what "others" would do. Notice that the HEB does not specify what those "others" are to be *like*. It does not ask her what a person she considers very wise and good would do. Just about "others" – with the subsurface implication that the choice which might be made by *any* "other" deserves consideration. Well, she probably knows that lots of "others" take that Liverpool ferry! And *every* "other" is regarded as a possible model by the HEB. The next step (page 130) is:

> Step Three: Evaluating the Alternatives
> Have you considered the consequences of each alternative – both direct and indirect?
> What personal goals do you want the solution to meet?
> What values are involved? Your own? Other people's?
> Have you personal preferences?
> What alternatives would give you the greatest emotional satisfaction?
> What factors have you no control over?
> What factors can you control?
> What external factors must be taken into account, e.g. amount of time, resources, etc.?
> What are the risks for each alternative?
> What are the probabilities for success?
> How will my decision affect other people?

Here again, objective right and wrong do not enter into consideration. First, the poor girl is asked to consider the "consequences of each alternative". But her distress is extreme precisely because she has been thinking about those "consequences" for several weeks, and the more she contemplates how awful it will be if she chooses one alternative (the right one) the more frightened, and therefore the more tempted, she is.

Then she is asked about her "personal goals" – the ones she "wants" the solution to meet. Again, objective morality is ignored, in favour of "personal" preference: her own chosen "goals"; her "wants". Unless this poor girl has already chosen "pleasing God", or even "doing the right thing" as her primary "personal goal" in life, this stuff about "personal goals" is going to weigh in heavily on the pro-abortion side.

With the next question it appears – for a fleeting moment or two! – that morality has at *last* come into consideration, when she is asked "What values are involved?" But remember, this girl has already (in that convent school) been put through lots and lots of "values clarification" sessions, so she knows that "values" are whatever she *chooses* to value, and one person's "values" are just as good as another's. So the HEB, in recalling "values" to her mind, is not necessarily bringing things like the sanctity of life into her mind. It all depends on what she *chooses* to regard as her own *personal* "values". And next, the HEB asks if the "values" involved here are really her own, or if they are "other people's". Well, which is it? Which of the many "values" which occur to her at this time will strike her as most "her own"? And which will strike her as "the Church's" values?

And then, right after this brief nod in the direction of "values", the HEB brings her right back to her "personal preferences" once again. She's been asked to consider her *personal* goals"; to think about whether the "values" involved are really her own *personal* ones; and now she is asked, "Have you personal preferences?"

And then, more of the same: she is asked which choice will give her "the greatest emotional satisfaction"! Well, what else would we expect, from emotivist Facilitators?

Then she has to consider what factors she can "control" – in two questions, one after the other. Will this call to her mind the fact that there are feminists around (some of them eager to "advise" her, too!) who make much of a "woman's right to control her own body"? The HEB certainly wants her to have "control" on her mind, to ask the same question *twice*, here. Why?

But that's not the only harm in that word "control", for people in acute temptation. My own experience of temptation is that it is a state in which I am excruciatingly aware of the fact that doing the right thing will involve some sort of submission of my will to God's will. It very often happens that the essence of the temptation is my desire to have my own way; that is, to have "control" over things. The "model" we really ought to have before our minds is the One who said, "Not My will but Thine be done". All this emphasis on "control" runs counter to our thinking thus. The HEB is really telling this child to say, "Not Thy will, but *mine* be done; I want to control my own life!"

There was another girl once, faced with a choice about an unexpected pregnancy. She didn't talk about "control", however. She called herself the

66

"slave of the Lord" instead. She voluntarily relinquished "control".

Not one question so far has focussed our young chooser's mind on anything likely to increase her fortitude – yet fortitude (and humility) are what she chiefly requires. But several questions have made her think about things which would make her even more frightened than she was at the start of these "steps" – if that were possible. Isn't that odd, for a set of questions meant to help people to make moral choices? Since after all, the really demanding moral choices require the exercise of considerable courage? As C. S. Lewis put it in the *Screwtape Letters*,

> courage is not simply *one* of the virtues, but the form of every virtue at the testing point, which means, at the point of highest reality. A chastity or honesty or mercy which yields to danger will be chaste or honest or merciful only on conditions. Pilate was merciful till it became risky.

And as for humility, not one of the questions so far has asked her to consider if she might be faced with her particular choice because of her own weakness. In fact none of the questions suggests in any way that she might *be* weak. They rather encourage her to fantasise herself strong, competent, very much in charge of things – like some top executive deciding whether or not to amalgamate with another company.

Next, she has to consider the "probabilities for success". Doesn't the word "success" have remarkably worldly connotations? I mean, when it is what a person facing a *moral* choice is told to consider? Which brings us to the last item in Step Three: the one one about how her decision will "affect other people". Notice, first of all, the fact that the HEB puts no moral imperative into this question. It does *not* ask her whether her decision might *harm* anyone else. It poses the question in a neutral, dispassionate manner. Second, note that this is the *last* question in this series, and the last question she must consider before the decision is made. The HEB left her a long time before bringing in how her actions might affect others; didn't it? Apparently, other people are not supposed to be a *priority* consideration when we make moral choices!

But that's not all, I think. You and I, if we are pro-lifers (and I rather suspect most readers of this book will be!) are in the habit of thinking of unborn children as people. (We do this because we are *realists*!) But will this girl have that habit of mind? What are the odds on it? So her child may not even occur to her, when she reads this question. It may well be that when she reads "other people" here, she merely thinks about her parents, and her boyfriend. And she knows very well that if she chooses to do the right thing, that choice will necessitate some pain for both parents and boyfriend (sadness for them at the knowledge of her past behaviour; fear of exposure for him). So this question, which at first seemed somewhat pro-

mising from a moral point of view, turns out only to increase her temptation – like the other questions. Step Four (page 130) comes next:

Step Four: Make the Decision
        Have you selected the best alternative in the light of the
           other steps?
        Have you reviewed it to see if it meets your objectives?

Obviously there's no look-in for objective right and wrong there! The word
"best" appears, but is instantly qualified by those "other steps" – which
had nothing to do with good and bad, right and wrong, true and false. So
"best" simply means "personally preferable", in this context. Next comes
Step Five (page 130):

Step Five: Implement the Decision
        Have you a plan to carry out the decision?
        Do you wish to integrate it into your lifestyle?
        Have you considered any contingency measures?
        Are you prepared to accept the consequences?

That's all. Right to the last, the HEB *never* asks her to think about objective
standards of morality. If she wants to have that abortion; if she wants to
"integrate" this decision into her "lifestyle" – well, that's OK by them,
provided she's thought about the possibilities and is prepared to accept the
consequences. Which is only to be expected, after all; the HEB does not
believe that Facilitators should impose their "values" on other people. All
is "choice": autonomous, personal "choice", in pursuit of "personal
goals".

    Right after the Five Steps, the manual contains a half-page (130) headed
"Different Styles of Decision-Making". Here the HEB lists 14 "styles", in
its own characteristic way. The last "style" is the one it has just outlined
in the Five Steps, and we can tell by the kind of language it uses that this
is the only "style" it thinks acceptable. Number 14 reads:

Following a plan. Weighing the facts and possible consequences.
Consulting with oneself and others.

The other "styles" are all phrased so as to sound ridiculous. Some of them
actually are ridiculous, such as Number 1 ("On impulse. Without thinking") and Number 6 ("Leaving it to chance. Tossing a coin"). But others
are not inherently ridiculous, but are only made to appear so by the way
the HEB uses words.

    In the first chapter of this book we said that the HEB has no use for the
"standards of a normative rationality". That is, for the use of the rational

mind to measure ideas or behaviour by objectively-valid norms (which are usually, in practice, *moral* norms). Two of the "styles" the HEB scorns here involve the use of the rational mind, and one involves the sense of obligation we feel toward moral norms. Style Number 2 is about using the mind. Here is how the HEB phrases it:

> Slowly. Ponderously, thinking about it. Often leaving the decision until it is too late.

Quite clever with words; aren't they? To manage to make reason itself seem unreasonable? Here is Number 11, which also has to do with rationality:

> Using excessive logic. Not allowing other factors to impinge.

Just when, I wonder, does logic become "excessive"? When it doesn't give way to things like "personal goals", "personal preferences" and whatever would give us "the greatest emotional satisfaction"? Presumably, yes.

I said the HEB alludes to moral obligation in this list of "styles" – once. Here is how the HEB phrases this reference:

> Allowing guilt to be the overriding factor. Strong sense of "what ought to be done".

The word "ought" does not appear often in this manual, and whenever it does, it is treated just as it is in this "style": with contempt.

CHAPTER 9

The Bedfellow Phenomenon:
Those Quasi-Facilitators

This book is mostly about the thinking and public acts of the people we call "Facilitators". That, is those who are deliberately "facilitating" certain social changes of a most unChristian nature. But when we defined "Facilitator" in our first chapter, we also mentioned certain "Quasi-Facilitators": people, we said, who are at work mainly within the Church's education establishment. We said that some of those involved in these school programmes fall into the "quasi-Facilitator" class.

Having read thus far, you will now have a fair idea what these pro-grammes are like – if you accept that I have presented them accurately! If you are not sure whether I have done so, remember you can go to the Central Catholic Library (74 Merrion Square, Dublin 2) to read the programmes themselves, and thus see if your judgement tallies with mine. Of course, the programmes *should* be more readily available than that – but that is not *my* fault; is it?

If you accept that my presentation is fair, then you are faced with a whopping great puzzle: you wonder *how* so many Catholic religious and lay catechists can accept the use of programmes of this sort in Catholic schools. If, as I maintain, these programmes are rooted in, and also inculcate, a view of the human person from which the concept of intelligent moral responsibility is *absent*, then surely it is inconceivable that Catholic schools should use these programmes. Yet they *do* use them. And many catechists and religious use them with the utmost enthusiasm.

I have heard from parents who have gone to nun-principals to complain about these programmes, and been sent away with an assurance that the programmes are excellent, and their complaints unfounded. I have heard from priests who defend these programmes; who say the programmes are of immense *spiritual* benefit to the kids. And, like anyone else who makes a habit of reading such journals as *The Furrow*, I have read essays by Catholic religion teachers who recommend that their fellow-catechists adopt these programmes and/or take the HEB's teacher-training course. For instance, the January 1985 issue of *The Furrow* carried an article by W. Richard Maher in which Mr. Maher advised precisely that.

Mr. Maher uses many of the same arguments the HEB trainees learn in that "role-play" session. He goes on about the difficulty of examinations; about the fact that examinations favour the intelligent; about the competitiveness and authoritarianism of the school system. He does *not* allude to the fact that these programmes are principally criticised on *moral* grounds!

70

To read what he says, you would think the kind of criticism found in this book (which is *typical*) simply did not exist. You would think that all resistance to these programmes came from people like Crusty Old Principal.

Mr. Maher rejects the idea that the catechist's job is the *teaching* of *truths* such as the truths in the Creed, or the moral truths expressed in the Commandments. He believes that the proper job of the catechist is not to impart *knowledge* about God and His law, but rather to work upon the *emotional life* of the pupil. That is, Mr. Maher sees the catechist as a therapist, rather than a teacher. Religious education, he suggests, is not really *about* God, His actions, the way He saved man, or His law. For Mr. Maher, religious education is about the emotional and aesthetic lives of the pupils. Instead of teaching doctrines and trying to explain those doctrines so as to make them clear to the *minds* of the students, Mr. Maher thinks that catechetics

> moves into those areas of moral value, or emotional refinement, of spiritual dynamic where other subjects do not go. It teases out of thought into the non-cognitive area . . . Religious education tends towards the dynamic and open-ended . . . (and) inherently deals with levels of personal experience, of love, of aesthetic appreciation, of peak moments of insight.

Mr. Maher believes that his sort of teaching is "spiritual"; obviously, for Mr. Maher, "spirituality" consists in some peculiar combination of emotional and aesthetic experience. For him learning what the Lord actually *taught* (such as, "If you love Me, keep My Commandments"!) is quite beside the point.

In the section of his essay headed "The Teacher as Facilitator", Mr. Maher recommends once more that the teacher "go beyond the intellectual to the level of feeling and emotion". And then, he advises teachers who want to take this advice (that is, teachers who want to become therapists instead of catechists, and practice therapy during the RE class!) to take the HEB's teacher-training course: the *same* course I've told you about here. The teacher who prepares himself thus will learn the "skills of group facilitation", he says. He will become expert in "group dynamics". He will learn how to employ "exercises that build trust in the class group". These exercises are obviously the sort used in the Ógra Chorcaí programme:

> Most important are those exercises that build trust in the class group. Many co-operative games and exercises in this area involve an element of physical contact, an aspect of the person we rarely recognise in teaching. This building of an atmosphere of trust enables the sharing of feelings.

Mr. Maher knows exactly where these ideas of his come from, too! He recommends "the model of human development put forth by Abraham Maslow, a humanistic psychologist". He enthuses over "the insights of humanistic psychology". That the "humanistic" psychologists hold views about the human person, and about the existence of an objective moral order which are totally incompatible with Christianity does not deter him in the slightest. He says that catechists should learn "strategies of teaching" which derive from these sources, and goes on thus:

> Many voluntary organisations which deal with young people train their personnel in this kind of group work. The Health Education Bureau runs courses for teachers, under the title of Health Education.

His whole article is a strong plea that Catholic religion teachers take such teacher-training programmes, to enable them to transform religion teaching into "facilitation".

Yes; Mr. Maher is clearly recommending – as a *replacement* for standard catechetics – exactly the sort of programme offered by Ógra Chorcaí. And he is not unique. If you visit your nearest Veritas shop, you will find evidence there that many catechists must be taking such advice to heart. You will see shelf upon shelf of books by such "humanistic" psychologists as Carl Rogers and Abraham Maslow. You will find all of Sidney Simon's books on "values clarification", as well as other "values clarification" books very like Dr. Simon's – which were written by Catholic religious, and published by Catholic publishing houses! You will find all these in the catechetics and guidance-counselling sections, where surely most of them are bought by teachers.

Is it credible that those teachers only buy those books so as to learn about psychological and education theories and methods they would never think of using? Hardly! The overwhelming likelihood is that those books are used by those teachers as source-books, from which they cull "values clarification" and other exercises to use in class. And to use, often enough, on the children of people who would be utterly astonished – and scandalised – to learn what sort of exercises they were! It's quite a situation. How can it have come about?

The real answer – a philosophical one – to that question lies outside the scope of this book. I haven't space here (supposing I could do it!) to list and analyse the many false ideas about human nature and education which are now fashionable in Catholic education circles. Nor have I room to try to trace those ideas back to their origins in, on the one hand, the speculations of "humanistic" psychologists, and on the other hand, the ruminations of certain heterodox modern theologians. To do all that would require a large book – if not several.

However, I have space here to relate a few historical facts about the mechanism by which many teaching religious have come to accept such

72

thoroughly unCatholic ideas. The fact is, during the past 20 years or so many religious orders have actually *invited* "humanistic" psychologists into their communities, to re-form the psyches of the religious themselves. This is still going on, right here in Ireland. I myself recently attended an introductory lecture by a nun, meant to tell interested people about one of these "self-actualisation" programmes. The talk was given in a Catholic retreat centre, and almost everyone present was a nun or priest. The speaker had high praise for Carl Rogers, and even spoke with extreme approbation about the way Dr. Rogers had abandoned the doctrine of Original Sin which had been taught him during his Lutheran childhood.

Indeed he did abandon it! So did *all* the "humanistic" psychologists. They teach that man is born perfect, and only becomes imperfect because warping institutions, such as the family and the Church, get at him during childhood. That is why these programmes lay such stress on divorcing teenagers from both home and Church. As William Kirk Kilpatrick says, in *The Emperor's New Clothes*, Erich Fromm (another of those "humanistic" psychologists)

> once observed that if the doctrine of Original Sin were true, much of his own theory would be untenable. And William Coulson, a former associate of Carl Rogers, recently characterised the encounter movement as "fundamentally anti-Catholic and probably knowingly anti-Catholic on Rogers' part".

Group therapy sessions such as the one that nun was pushing have become commonplace in convents. And obviously, if nuns accept that such programmes are doing the sisters good (in spite of considerable evidence to the contrary!) then those nuns will also come to accept the view of man upon which such programmes are based. Including the characteristic rejection of Original Sin (with all that that implies); including the confusion of emotionality with spirituality; including the whole lot of it. Unless an individual nun is gifted with a highly analytic mind, and also has enough spare time to examine the presuppositions upon which the programme is based, she is unlikely to do otherwise.

That many nuns now seem to regard these psychologists as spiritual teachers (offering perhaps an alternative Gospel whereby we shall be saved?) has recently been attested by no less a personage than Cardinal Joseph Ratzinger, Prefect of the Sacred Congregation for the Doctrine of the Faith. In the *Ratzinger Report* (Fowler Wright, 1985) he is reported as deploring

> the entrance into the convents, at times wholly unexamined, of psychologies and psychoanalyses of different tendencies; all this has led to the burning problems of identity and, with many women, to the

73

collapse of motivations sufficient to justify religious life. Visiting a Catholic bookshop . . . I noticed that there (and not only there) the spiritual treatises of the past had been replaced by the widespread manuals of psychoanalysis. Theology had made way for psychology, where possible to the one most in vogue.

As a result, these programmes have gone through any number of religious orders, here and abroad, like a prairie fire. Leaving, sometimes, similar devastation in their wake. Dr. Kilpatrick tells the story of what happened to one teaching order in Los Angeles:

> In 1967 . . . Rogers and his colleagues at the Western Behavioural Science Institute were invited by the Immaculate Heart Order of Nuns to revitalise their extensive school system in the Los Angeles area. For the next two years the system, which included the Immaculate Heart College, several high schools, and a string of elementary schools, became the scene of intensive encounter and marathon group activity. One has to go back to the appearance of the devils in the convent of Loudon to find a more radical transformation of a group of Sisters. Within a short time the nuns had become humanised, feminised, and revolutionised. Not long after the departure of the WBSI people they cut their ties with the official Catholic Church.
>   William Coulson, one of the project leaders, later wrote: "When we started the project . . . there were six hundred nuns and fifty-nine schools: a college, eight high schools, and fifty elementary schools. Now, four years later as I write, a year following the formal completion of the project, there are two schools left and no nuns."

Such events, one might think, would give pause. But those who would replace religious formation and catechetics programmes with "facilitation" remain undeterred. Now, Dr. Kilpatrick – with whom I agree, obviously – says that religious knowledge must be imparted as we impart other bodies of firmly-established teaching: as *objective truths* accessible in some way to the mind, rather than as will-o-the-wispy "feelings" such as might emerge as a group "consensus" during a "facilitated" discussion:

> Now in many respects teaching Catholic/Christian faith is more like teaching a physics class than a social studies class. It has to do with immutable laws. One does not decide upon the validity of divine truths by the group discussion method any more than one uses that method to decide upon the point at which water boils.

The quasi-Facilitators clearly disagree, and think that religious truths will somehow *emerge* (through some special revelation?) if the kids are encouraged to sit in pairs and "share"; to caress one another's wrists while trying to feel "caring" feelings. How such goings-on could possibly reveal things like the doctrine of the Trinity I fail to see. But it *seems* to be what those who think like this *want*. They don't want explanations of doctrine; they want the kids put through "experiences" instead, from which "experiences" the kids are supposed to gather the truths.

Such recommendations presuppose, I think, that the one recommending has come to confuse the emotional with the spiritual, and has at the same time ceased to regard the intellect as a spiritual faculty. This confusion is one of the great problems of modern catechetics – partly because it is simply false, and one false supposition inevitably leads to a lot more false thinking; and partly because it is just the sort of supposition which gives the greatest opportunity to the being who, St. Peter has assured us, goes about like a roaring lion, seeking whom he may devour.

Those who confuse the emotional and spiritual, and demote the rational to a sub-spiritual plane, also tend to mix up the theological virtue of charity with mere affectionate feelings; that is, with *liking*. The two things are, of course, not at all the same – as Catholic teachers and apologists always used to hasten to point out. One such who *still* says it, God bless him, is Mgr. A. N. Gilbey, who makes the distinction beautifully in *We Believe*:

> Charity requires an act of will on our part, by which we love God above all things and our neighbour as ourselves for God's sake. That needs to be constantly emphasised, because Charity, or love – and they are synonymous in the New Testament – is, as you know, nowadays generally spoken of as though it were an intense and passionate form of liking. So we need to distinguish between liking and loving, which are two completely different things.
>
> Liking lies in the feelings, the feelings which we can so little control, or at most control indirectly. We cannot help but like certain persons, things, places and occupations. Liking is an entirely instinctive reaction on our part. Since it is entirely instinctive, there can be no virtue in it . . . We can do something to educate and change our feelings to some extent, but ultimately liking is an instinctive activity for which we cannot really be held morally responsible.
>
> Now, loving is completely and absolutely different to liking. By love we understand sinking our will in the will of the beloved. That is what love means – to will what the one you love wills. That, of course, is why love is the greatest of all the virtues. Plainly, if you can get love and liking to coincide, so very much the easier. It is much easier to love the things which we like. But if you cannot get them to coincide, do not worry at all. You and I will never be judged by what we have liked or disliked. We shall be judged for all eternity by what we have loved, by the use we have made of our will, by whether we have chosen the

object of our love aright when we have sunk our will in the will of another person (pages 192-193).

That long quotation comes out of a completely different doctrine of man from the one at the root of such "facilitation" programmes as our Catholic quasi-Facilitators recommend. The kids would *never* get that sort of doctrine from the "experiences" Mr. Maher, the HEB, and Ógra Chorcaí give them. They would get exactly the opposite idea: that charity is a matter of warm "feelings", which "feelings" we should try to express by fondling one another, "caringly".

Does Mr. Maher *want* the kids to get such false ideas? I certainly hope not. I hope Mr. Maher wants the kids to give their free intellectual assent (not merely an emotional acquiescence) to the truth of all Catholic teaching. I hope Mr. Maher has no idea that the sort of programme he recommends might have the practical effect of "facilitating" kids right into the Well Woman Centre, and from thence on to that Liverpool ferry. But whether he desires that outcome or not, I think the kind of teaching he prefers *will* "facilitate" it.

As an obvious example of the sort of class exercise which could "facilitate" abominations, consider the "values clarification" device of the "survival game". This exercise is one of those most commonly found in these programmes. It is in the Ógra Chorcaí handbook, on pages 30-31. It also forms part of the North Western Health Board's "Lifeskills" programme. I know it does because a parent told me. This parent attended an evening presentation, conducted by a NWHB Facilitator who put the parents through some of the exercises in the school programme. This "survival game" was among them.

The "game" exists in several versions, but the basics are always the same. The kids are asked to pretend that they are in some life-or-death emergency situation in which only *some* people (usually six out of ten) can be saved. Then they are given a few facts (age, occupation, etc.) about those wanting to live, and asked to decide which of them to exclude from the fallout shelter. They are asked to make their decisions of the basis of the relative "value" of these desperate people. The standard is *strictly* utilitarian.

The parent who told me about this exercise said that in the session he attended, one parent tried to get the Facilitator to allow the group to use the "Titanic solution": that is, to try to save the weakest first (while the rest recommended themselves to their Maker and the orchestra played "Nearer My God to Thee"!). That is, this parent tried to interest this Facilitator in the approach to this problem which was taken for granted as *right* in western society only such a short time ago as 1912, when the Titanic went down.

The Facilitator simply wouldn't have it. She insisted that the selection be made on the basis of which people were most "valuable". That is, she

76

required a solution based on a strictly utilitarian ethic.

Dr. Kilpatrick says that putting kids through that sort of exercise (and these programmes are absolutely choc-a-bloc with exercises like that one!) results in a "gradual erosion of proper moral sentiments". He goes on,

> Habituation is a fact of life as surely in our time as it was in Aristotle's. The difference perhaps is that only the advertisers, the media, and the promoters still recognise that fact. This gives them an enormous advantage over the naive majority, who cling piously to the belief that values are somehow self-created when, in fact, their values are the playthings of the desensitisers. For desensitisation is the engine of the current moral upheaval. Thirty years ago, C. S. Lewis contemplated the possibility of an "abolition of man" – an alteration of human nature that would remove man's moral nature. The first step would be a deconditioning process, "the stifling of all deep-set repugnancies".

I think these "health education" programmes (like the rest of the "facilitation" we are getting from government, media, etc.) all serve to stifle those repugnancies. And in among the Facilitators doing this stifling, we find apparently-well-meaning Catholic educators: quasi-Facilitators who seem to have swallowed "humanistic" psychology whole – without so much as a moral hiccup.

Please don't misunderstand me. I am *not* saying that catechists like Mr. Maher *want* to encourage abominations, such as programmes for euthanasia or for aborting the handicapped. But I am saying that if we had a government trying to bring in an Amendment to allow such things (and don't forget: our present government seems to have sanctioned the idea of leaving room in our Constitution for aborting handicapped children, and only abandoned the idea when it saw that the public would not accept it!) would it not prefer that those who were to vote had had their deep-set repugnancies to such ideas quietly stifled, when they were in school? In desensitising school programmes, which got those voters-to-be well used to the idea (repugnant, of course, at *first*) that the "less valuable" should be liquidated?

During the run-up to the vote for the Pro-Life Amendment, I went to Lough Derg. While there I talked to a charming, intelligent and devout young woman: a post-graduate student at an Irish university, who was on her fourth visit to Lough Derg. Not unnaturally, we eventually got to the subject of the Amendment. She was against it.

I naturally assumed that she opposed it because she thought the wording defective. After all, she was a devout Catholic; wasn't she? One who had "done" Lough Derg four times? So I was stunned when she calmly replied that no, she didn't think the wording defective. It was just that she believed in aborting the handicapped.

77

When I got my breath back, I asked her if she didn't see some element of contradiction in her being at Lough Derg, considering that she was not a Catholic believer. She was astonished – obviously quite *sincerely* horrified – that anyone could say such a thing about her! So I put it to her that there really *is* such a thing as Catholic moral teaching, and that she had rejected it. I told her that she couldn't call herself a Catholic believer, if she had ceased to believe that the Church teaches truth.

She absolutely rejected my argument – on the grounds that no one had *ever* suggested such an outrageous idea to her before! Why, she said, she was a very good Catholic. She had gone to Catholic schools all her life. She went to Mass every Sunday. She had participated enthusiastically in many retreats. She even went to Confession. She was as good a Catholic as anybody! And furthermore, she said, getting into her stride, she hadn't taken her position on aborting the handicapped *casually*.

No, she said; she had *thought it over*. She had considered the alternatives. She had throught about the consequences for everybody involved. She hadn't just decided willy-nilly. She was quite sure that her solution was the *best* one for her, so of course she could hold it in good conscience! So how *dare* I come along and say she had to choose between believing in aborting the handicapped, and being a Catholic?

Now, what sort of religious education had that young woman received, do you think? She isn't stupid. She's a post-graduate student, with an excellent degree behind her. And she's a very nice girl too. If only someone had told her of the existence of Catholic doctrine, I suspect that she would have decided that on this point the Church was wiser than she was. But, apparently, no one *had* told her. She just didn't *know* that there are certain teachings one must accept if one is to consider oneself a Catholic. The nuns in her convent school must have given her "values clarification" and other "facilitation" instead of doctrine.

Sometimes, young people react in the opposite way when, many years later than they *should* have been told, they discover the existence of Catholic doctrine. David Noel Doyle, writing in the *Ballintrillick Review* (February 1986) tells about a young man at UCD, who attended a recent Newman Association meeting addressed by a bishop. When question time came around, this young man stood up and said, among other things, "I'm 21 and I discover there is such a thing as doctrine, and serious sin. *And no one told me*. I am very angry."

Those who replace catechetics with "facilitation" have a lot to answer for, I think. Let us hope that presently they will see their mistake, and leave "facilitation" with the HEB, SERR, the IFPA, the IPPF and their ilk. That is where it belongs. *Oremus.*

CHAPTER 10

* "Busy Phantoms"

On 7 September 1983 the people of Ireland voted in a referendum on a proposal to amend the Irish Constitution by the addition of an article designed by its proponents to protect the lives of unborn children from induced abortion.

When on 8 September the votes were counted, it was found that the majority of those casting their ballot had accepted the proposal, which ran:

> The State acknowledges the right to life of the unborn, and, with due regard to the equal right to life of the mother, guarantees in its laws to respect, and, as far as practicable, by its laws to defend and vindicate that right.

The effect of what came to be called the Pro-Life Amendment was to strengthen the provisions of the Offences Against the Person Act (1861) which, though it provided for punishment by law of those, including the mother, who might either attempt to procure or succeed in procuring an abortion, did not specifically recognise the right to life of the child in question. It could – and looked as if it would – have been repealed within a few years. The way would then have been open for the provision of abortion clinics in this country as in Britain where, in the absence of constitutional protection, the same 1861 Act had been superseded by the Abortion Act of 1967, despite the existence of the Infant Life Preservation Act (1929) which forbids the destruction of an infant capable of being born alive.

Between July 1980 and September 1983 this country witnessed an unprecedented public debate, fanned by a hostile media which portrayed the proposed Amendment as a threatened right-wing political coup – when its proponents seemed to be gaining ground. When it was felt that the public might simple be persuaded to ignore the Amendment, the alternative pictures were of a storm in a teacup or an undignified dogfight.

Many a bewildered voter on the street repeatedly questioned the need for a Pro-Life Amendment. Many castigated "society" for its apparently uncaring attitude to women in difficulties. Some dismissed the Amendment Campaign arguments by saying that if their daughter were pregnant they

*Lesbian Feminism. "We were very busy phantoms". Irish Women Speak Out. A Plan of Action from the National Women's Forum. Produced by the Council for the Status of Women. Published by Co-op Books Ltd., Dublin, 1981. P. 54.

79

would be only too willing to pay for an abortion, or otherwise assist her in having one.

Few asked why abortion had become such a topical subject in Ireland all of a sudden. Fewer still either knew or cared about the organisations which had sprung up in our country precisely to promote abortion. The existence of these had sown the seed of the pro-life movement, which in turn had given birth to the proposed Amendment. And some - in particular a few members of the Catholic clergy - apparently wished that the subject had never been tackled, and might have attempted to bury at least one strand of the pro-life movement had it not been forthright and determined to succeed. Perhaps the message of the last 20 years, aimed at re-awakening in the laity the concept of themselves as "Church" had finally been absorbed by some at least of the 97 per cent Catholic population of the State - ironically, to the chagrin of some members of the hierarchy!

*   *   *   *   *

The scene had been set in 1975, designated International Women's Year by the United Nations Commissioner on the Status of Women. In that year at a conference held in Mexico City, a Plan of Action was decided upon. Then the UN sponsored a Decade for Women (1976-1985). In July 1980 the second UN World Conference of Women was held in Copenhagen. Its main objectives were to review the 1975 Plan of Action and to consider a Programme of Action to cover the second half of the decade. The main themes of the latter were Equality, Development and Peace. Between 1975 and 1980 the emphasis was switched to the "sub themes" of the proposed conference so that Employment, Health and Education became the prominent items on the agenda. Being a member of the UN, Ireland sent an official delegation to Copenhagen, accompanied by advisers. The delegation, led by the Minister of State at the Department of Labour, comprised five government representatives - three from the Department of Labour and two from Foreign Affairs. The advisers were two members of the Council for the Status of Women, the Chairperson of the Employment Equality Agency and a member of the Health Education Bureau. After two weeks' discussion, the Copenhagen conference produced a World Plan of Action.

On returning home the members of the Council for the Status of Women who had attended both the UN Conference and a rival Forum - also held in Copenhagen - formed a committee chaired by Dr. Hazel Boland. They planned a National Forum along the lines of the Copenhagen model. Thus it was that the National Women's Forum, called to formulate a National Plan of Action "specifically relevant to Ireland"[1] and "for presentation to the Government"[2] was held at the RDS on 15 and 16 November 1980. Among the invited speakers was Dr. Lucille Mair, Secretary-General of the

1980 World Conference of the Decade of Women, who lauded the organisers for producing the first "governmental follow-up meeting"[3] to the World Conference – which, she noted, held "special significance".[4]

Workshops led by Facilitators (*their* word!) were organised to deal with Health, Education, Employment, Law, Rural Development, Women in Conflict Situations, Media and Communications/Networking. The organisation of the workshops into small groups, heavily biased by Facilitators already convinced of the logic of the proposals, was the key to success. The report of the Forum produced by the Council for the Status of Women states that it was "definitely an organisational mistake to . . . attempt to conduct a discussion with more than 20 people present"[5] . . . This referred to the group discussion on the topic of "Church Control of Education" (the title ". . . chosen by the Council Planning Committee"[6] and dealt with under the umbrella of Women and Education) which had apparently produced an unsatisfactory outcome as far as the Facilitators were concerned.

The participants at the Forum were addressed by Mr. Charles J. Haughey, then Taoiseach, and by President Hillery. The report on the proceedings noted that "participation by the Irish Government at this level represented a very clear acknowledgement of its interest in the Plan of Action".[7] In acknowledging Government financial assistance it claimed that the "breadth of planning" for the Forum "would have been difficult otherwise".[8]

The World Plan of Action was, according to the Council, very relevant to Ireland since, among its many priorities was that of improving the conditions of women in rural areas. Ireland was referred to as a largely rural country whose economy "*is dependent upon international finance for industrialisation*" . . . and as such, the possibilities of the programme were ". . . *highly relevant to the Irish situation*".[9] Among the Forum's proposals, compiled by the Council in its report entitled "Irish Women Speak Out" were the following.

HEALTH

The repeal of the 1979 Family Planning Act on the grounds that it restricted availability of contraceptives and discriminated against poor women.
Free sterilisation of women on demand.
The decriminalisation of abortion.
The abolition of the status of illegitimacy.
The provision of State-funded creche facilities.
The recognition of the offence of rape within marriage and the setting up of local authority grant-aided rape crisis centres.

EDUCATION

The abolition of what is termed "sexism" – i.e. role identification with respect to sex, in education, with the demand that teacher training include input on the topic. Progress would be monitored by a Government-funded National Committee under the auspices of the Council.

Payment for child rearing at home.

Secular control of education under "parent or teacher power".[10] The establishment of the right of teachers to opt out of the teaching of religion.

Sex education for all students beginning at *primary* level and including "remedial and slow learners"; giving top priority to the "physically and mentally disabled".[11]

LAW

Marriage preparation courses at second level which should "not . . . be part of a religious education".[12]

The raising of the legal age of marriage from 16 years to 18 years.

Legal action to challenge the existing laws on prostitution.

The adoption of legitimate children.

The LESBIAN WOMEN'S GROUP contribution included the following:

The end of Catholic control of education in Ireland;

a national programme covering sexuality – and lesbianism in particular – for schools, community health centres and the media;

a charter of children's rights, to include the right to "freedom of sexual expression";[13]

divorce on request;

absolute protection for lesbians at work in what were termed "self-governing" institutions – e.g. hospitals, the church and other services.[14]

While there are injustices in Irish law, and women do suffer as a result, one might be forgiven for asking if a clean sweep of all existing institutions – including the Catholic Church – would improve matters. Whether recognised or not the trend, in the light of the deliberations of the Women's Forum, does seem to be towards the abolition, or at least the metamorphosis, of much that is currently familiar to and cherished by the average Irish citizen.

Why did all of this come about? In particular, how did the subject of abortion come to occupy so much of the national debating time for almost three years? To understand, one must address oneself to the philosophy and the origins of the anti-life movement.

1 . . . 14. *Irish Women Speak Out. A Plan of Action from the National Women's Forum*. Co-op Books Ltd., Dublin, 1981.

CHAPTER 11

The Philosophy of the Anti-Life Movement

It has been argued that abortion is not new; that it is a practice as old as history. While this may be true, one cannot help wondering whether the unprecedented increase in the number of abortions in our time does not indicate that man is attempting to play God – preoccupied as he is with destruction by abortion on the one hand, and creation on the other, via the techniques of in vitro fertilisation, surrogacy and cross-breeding of mankind with other species. It would hardly be prophetic, under the circumstances, to surmise that the end product of the divorce of sex from pro-creation would be a society in which sexual roles had been abolished in favour of a neutered asexual being, socially programmed by a new theory of education. The mobility of this *It* within the workforce would be enormous. Offspring would, of course, have to be provided to replace wastage. Such workers as were needed could be produced in "crops" to be grown periodically in laboratories from the seed of subjects specially selected for breeding because of their genetic superiority. They could be reared in creches and "processed" through the education system much like tins of peas. Yet another batch – albeit a well-educated, socially- and politically-acceptable cadre of workers – would be available to the masters of destiny. State expenditure on worn-out subjects could be reduced by encouraging those socially-motivated people to do their final duty to society and quietly take their leave of it when their computer number came up. State aid, in the form of specially-trained and compassionate "carers" would assist those who found the process difficult.

We are surely a great deal closer now to Aldous Huxley's vision than when he wrote *Brave New World* more than half a century ago. It is therefore worth reminding ourselves, that although when men went to the moon the theory of its being made of green cheese and inhabited by a friendly old man was finally exploded, *so too was the very notion of the impossibility of getting there!*

What is significant about abortion today is the *scale* of the phenomenon. Never before have governments decreed that abortion be allowed as of right. Never have so many abortions been recorded worldwide – an estimated 55 million *per annum*. Never until this century have governments dictated how many children couples will be permitted to have. Never until our own day have abortion and sterilisation become compulsory (as in some countries in given circumstances); nor has the cost to the State of rearing those whom the last generation of our countrymen so aptly called *duine le*

Dia been measured as against the cost of their elimination. For the first time in history this century has witnessed the reversal of the maxim that the State was made to serve man. It is becoming increasingly clear that the State, in many instances, has become a machine which has outgrown its creator, to the extent that man is now its servant – in some instances almost its off-spring – and is endowed with a single value: that of his economic worth.

The philosophical roots of today's thinking on abortion and inter-related subjects have been attributed by John Powell in his *Abortion: the Silent Holocaust* to the Hegelian principle of utility and Dewey's philosophy of atheistic humanism. John Dewey's tenet of "learning by doing" has had an enormous impact on 20th century education, especially in the United States. Whereas his ideas were useful in the teaching of practical subjects, they were entirely unsuited to the field of ethics – the science of how one ought to behave. Though in the practical field experimentation may be legitimate, in the ethical field such experimentation creates situation ethics. The latter, following Dewey, simply means that there are no fixed principles upon which to reflect before decision making, since each situation is unique and the principles applied to the solution of a problem in the first instance need not be applied to its solution the next time round. The ability to solve the problem is all that matters to Dewey. Educationalists in the United States, reaping the rewards of Dewey's thinking, are beginning to change tactics. Dewey, however, has only recently crossed the Atlantic and landed in Ireland; no doubt to sojourn here until, in time-honoured fashion, we make our own mistakes before sending him home.

Donald de Marco in *Abortion in Perspective: The Rose Palace or the Fiery Dragon?*[1] traces the origin of the present abortion phenomenon "suddenly and overwhelmingly . . . convinced of the importance of ecological balances on the subhuman level"[2] . . . to several philosophies from the Greek Democritus to the present upsurge of sociologism. From the belief of Democritus in the importance of the individual atom is derived the emphasis on the exclusive rights of the individual woman, as expressed in the current claim to sovereignty of the woman over not only her fertility, but over its results: i.e. a child. "Viewed atomistically, the individual man presents a very small case indeed *vis-à-vis* society. In the same way the developing foetus or embryo appears to present a very small case compared to the individual rights of the mother . . . Likewise if the rights of the individual are to be measured quantitively against the needs and pressures of society, there can be no serious disagreement. The individual must go."[3]

Descartes' theory of "I think, therefore I am" is used by those who contend that personhood is dependent, not on the universal natural capacity of humans to think, but on the actual measured capacity of the individual to do so. Such philosophy can conveniently be used to write off those who, in the opinion of other human beings, are either not yet able to think; or who have, through accident or disease, apparently lost the ability to do so.

85

This stance conveniently supports the elimination of both the unborn and of those deemed to have ceased to function in what society would regard as a "meaningful" way. It denies the reality of individual capacity, substituting a supposed norm. But if both our different-sized glasses are full, can you claim that your pint glass of stout is fuller than my tumbler of gin and tonic?

Then there is existentialism, based on the notion that man is an "existence" who by his own freely-chosen actions continuously strives to achieve his zenith or "essence". This presumes humanity to be "an achievement, not an endowment",[4] thus supporting the notion that one can somehow become *more* human. If that be the case, there are no grounds for believing all men to have been created equal, and governments might quite rightly make one law for the born and another for the unborn. If men are not equal from the first moment of their existence (i.e. conception, viz. fertilisation) at what arbitrary point do they become so?

The dictum "seeing is believing" of the empiricist is variously interpreted by realists, pragmatists, utilitarians and positivists and translated into up-to-the-minute situation ethics. Applied to the foetus it is used to describe a being with whom an adult cannot "visually identify",[5] especially in the early stages of foetal development. It became the basis for the denial of the humanity of the foetus and his relegation to the status of a mere "blob of jelly". Finally it became the cornerstone of sociologism. Since no man is an island, runs its argument, it follows that he must somehow be "humanised" by society. The process relies on the assumption that the unborn child who has yet to come into contact with society is "pre-human" and his life is therefore expendable. It labels as sub-human those who either cannot or do not conform to contemporary society's theory of "human-ness". It is further extended to prop up the argument that "unwanted" children are a danger to society because they are doomed to being reared in homes psychologically unprepared for them, and are therefore more likely to become delinquent. Better to be aborted than to be delinquent!

Philosophy does not reveal truths to serve us,
but truth for us to serve.

—Jacques Maritain.

The philosophical base on which a society is founded is crucial to the broad ethic adopted by its people, on which its laws depend. The philosophy on which Irish society is based, considers man an indivisible integration of body, soul and mind; a created being owing homage to an Almighty and placed within a cosmos ordered by observable physical laws. Irish society has, in addition, for 1500 years now based its way of life on the Judaeo-Christian philosophy – the main tenet of which continues to be love of God and love of neighbour. In ethical terms this translates into "do unto others as you would be done by". Fundamental to love of neighbour must surely be respect for his right to exist. This raises the question: how could a society which professes in its fundamental law to cherish all its children – and equally at that – discard the basis of such respect and adopt for itself laws which would allow for the antithesis? For how can it be argued that one can love one's neighbour and simultaneously facilitate his elimination? Unless, of course, the philosophy underlying that civilisation has been hijacked.

Hijacking is a commonplace phenomenon nowadays and something feared by so-called civilised societies. In a hijack, the driver of the vehicle is directed, by the use of force, to take a new route and arrive wherever the hijacker so directs. Usually, bargaining produces a compromise devised to avoid death, injury, or other misdeed; and if it is adopted, everybody who has survived the ordeal eventually gets home carrying the marks of the experience with them, probably for life. But what of society? Is it possible that its philosophical cornerstone can be snatched from it? Yes! And when this happens, the ethic which governs the day-to-day dealings of man with neighbour must necessarily change in order to take account of the new philosophy ushered in like a new regime. In order to woo a society to a radical change in its philosophy it is necessary to induce its philosophers to espouse new thinking, or to re-promulgate outdated models and then persuade the populace to adopt the update.

Such an attempt was made here from the Department of Philosophy at University College, Cork. In a Thomas Davis Lecture delivered in 1981, Dr. Dolores Dooley Clarke, a lecturer in medical ethics, fired the first shot. She was described by the *Irish Times* of 11 September 1981 as an American and the product of a "progressive Catholic convent which encouraged intellectual independence" . . . Such intellectual independence in a confessed Catholic apparently helped Dr. Dooley Clarke to argue in favour of abortion while simultaneously "respecting human life". In the following quotation, taken from an extract of the Thomas Davis Lecture reprinted by the *Irish Times* Dr. Dooley Clarke stated her position thus:

> I have argued that a general prohibition on abortion is justified with three exceptions to this prohibition: where the life of the mother is threatened, where the pregnancy is the result of rape and where deformity of the foetus is such that there is no developing potential (*sic*) to be a living human being.

Noting that no legislation had been enacted in Ireland to "modify the strict prohibition on abortion" of the 1861 Offences Against the Person Act, Dr. Dooley Clarke suggested a . . . "revision of the law which would specify some legal exceptions within an overall prohibition on abortion".

As we shall see, that was exactly the kind of Pro-Life Amendment Dr. Garret FitzGerald favoured – a sort of have-your-cake-and-eat-it approach. Summing up her argument Dr. Dooley Clarke conceded:

> Few legislators and certainly few moralists would contend that it is an easy task to devise *a just and humane abortion law* . . . which does not put us on the much dreaded "slippery slope" of abortion on demand.

In the wake of such statements the *Irish Times* – ever the champion of the liberal – commended Dr. Dooley Clarke for what it called her "intellectual poise while under attack from those who see her ideas as dangerously radical" . . .

Following the utterances of the Lecturer in Medical Ethics, the head of the Department, Louvain Alumnus Rev. Professor Brendan O'Mahony took up the cause. While strongly opposed to abortion, he argued that as a philosopher, and following some of the great Western philosophers, it was possible to admit to the case for abortion as argued by Dr. Dooley Clarke. Presumably, Professor O'Mahony was unaware that the exceptions advanced were the classic pro-abortionists' trilogy. Nor was it the first time that a Catholic clergyman had been used to further abortionists' arguments. Bernard Nathanson in his book *Aborting America* documents the use and abuse of Catholic clergy during the abortion campaign in the United States. The strategy there – as here – was to re-hash mediaeval thinking about the philosophical questions of ensoulment and personhood, with the sole object of confusing people. It succeeded in America.

Stated simply, some mediaeval philosophers held that the foetus was not human until its form could be clearly seen, and that it did not receive its soul until the body was formed, and therefore not for some time after conception. This meant that abortion was not considered homicide until the foetus could clearly be distinguished. This argument is therefore conveniently used – along with others – to justify abortion in the case of conception occurring after rape. In addition, the application of Descartes' dictum *"cogito ergo sum"* as applied to the notion of personhood implies that a foetus, though ensouled, but devoid of a fully-formed brain, cannot be considered a human person – though its form is clearly evident. Such a notion facilitates abortion in the case of obvious physical deformity, regardless of how long the child is expected to survive.

However, the inconsistencies in the arguments were readily perceived by the majority of Irish people who voted on the issue. Only on stage in the world of make-believe could one wear two hats, and even there not simultaneously. Furthermore, it is illogical to accept the deliberate sacrifice of defenceless human life in *in utero* unless society accepts that life at *any* stage from conception to old age can be sacrificed.

In summary, to alter the accepted philosophy of a society is to provoke ethical change, and ethics govern how we ought to treat one another. The fact that other Western countries have adopted a materialistic philosophy, with its utilitarian ethic, ought not to be sufficient reason for Ireland to do so. If France can worry about the metamorphosis of its language to *"franglais"* – and the hijacking of its culture in the process – have we not sufficient reason to be concerned about the change in direction to which our society is currently subject? Or are we also quietly acquiescing in the death of our culture and its ethic? Are we being facilitated into a New Ireland? For all that is required for the painless transition from here to there are

". . . mutations irresistibly wrought in the structure of consciousness by science and technique".[6]

1. De Marco, Donald. *Abortion in Perspective. The Rose Palace or the Fiery Dragon?* Hayes Publishing Co., Ohio, USA, 1974.
2. *Ibid.*
3. *Ibid.*
4. *Ibid.*, quoting Sartre.
5. *Ibid.*
6. Gehlen, Arnold. *Man in the Age of Technology.* Translated by Patricia Lipscomb. Columbia University Press, New York, 1980.

CHAPTER 12

Some Thoughts for St. Valentine's Day

Blest are they who do not see
Death upon the family,
Friend in trouble, stolen wife,
Ruin of the nation's life.

—*The Panchatantra*[1]

It's 14 February 1985 – St. Valentine's Day. The Dáil is in session and TDs are discussing whether to debate an amendment to the Health (Family Planning) Act 1979 today, or to postpone the debate for another week. It is a blustering cold day outside. The Bill, introduced by Mr. Barry Desmond, Minister for Health and member of the Irish Family Planning Association, an affiliate of the International Planned Parenthood Federation, proposes to alter the present situation to allow the sale of non-medical contraceptives to people aged 18 and over, regardless of marital status. It is proposed that in future these contraceptives will be on sale at pharmacies, health board clinics, maternity hospitals and family planning outlets.

It is said by the proponents that the measure, if adopted, will regularise the present situation and in addition, help to mitigate the ridicule directed at the nation which in 1979 apparently found and adopted "an Irish solution to an Irish problem". Such is our collective national inferiority complex that though we can urge the populace to Buy Irish – on the assumption that what we buy will be as good as, if not better than, imported competitors – we cannot, it seems, be allowed to produce home-grown solutions to our Irish problems. We must instead be persuaded to believe that we are the laughing stock of Europe before we can be induced, ever so gently, to make a "minor" change in a law such as this. Nobody, of course, would be so foolish as to dare state that minor changes in legislation can have major consequences; nobody, that is, except those who are prepared to suffer yet more ridicule and derision from the self-proclaimed prophets of enlightenment.

Yet, as Simone Veil, *Facilitateuse* and former President of the European Parliament noted in an interview to the *Irish Times* on 3 March 1975:

> My great passion is the law, insofar as it reflects human realities. By modifying it, you can modify the whole pattern of human behaviour.

It is a curious paradox that Mme. Veil, who survived just such an experiment in law-changing at the hands of the Nazis, should have such views on social engineering. She was invited to share her views on the implementation of abortion and contraception laws with the Irish nation, courtesy of the Women's Political Association, in Dublin some years later when the abortion movement here needed a veneer of respectability. On that occasion Mme. Veil, whom the *Irish Times* inimitably described as "the architect of France's abortion laws" speaking in French (her English is poor) told the WPA meeting in Jury's Hotel on 28 November 1981 that there were now so many abortions done in France that free access to contraception and more sex education were the answer: and that in any case, the demand for such from young people was overwhelming.

*   *   *   *   *

A little thing will lift him high
A little make him fall;
Twixt balance-beam and scamp there is
No difference at all.[2]

Though the air outside the Dáil Chamber is bitterly cold, TDs' temperatures and those of a very large number of their constituents are above average for the time of year. There is much talk of pressure from constituents anxious to let the men and women for whom they voted know that they – the constituents – pay the piper and so must have a say in calling the tune. It seems there is quite a discord between payer and piper just now. Indeed, Mr. Dessie O'Malley TD has gone so far as to say that the debate is not about contraception but about the concept of who should rule the country. Poor man, he must have forgotten that the *people* do, of course, in a democracy; and in any case they are merely reminding those whom they have elected to vote for them, precisely of that fact.

Back in the chamber two rival groups are being called to order to orchestrate the piece, both conducted with the use of whips rather than batons. Occasionally the more experienced or senior, or even virtuoso players attempt a solo act, only to be drowned out at the behest of the whip. A few are contemplating leaving the show but are naturally anxious about keeping their audience in future. Solo acts are difficult to organise.

All players know that their jobs depend on playing party music, a pleasant enough occupation when one's instrument is kept in tune. Those whose instruments go out of the tune must suffer a penalty. To alter our metaphor, they are obliged to entertain their colleagues, and invited guests, together with whatever audience can be garnered by the media, by publicly walking a tightrope. On this occasion, as it happens, the rope has been greased with a slippery substance called "conscience". Some TDs, when asked if they noticed any tendency to slide one way or another, confessed that they were so busy trying to get the ordeal over that they didn't notice

91

the grease. Others claimed that the crowds urging them to weigh up the dangers (there are no safety nets for professional tightrope walkers) only made them more determined than ever. More felt that the crack of the party whip tended to propel them in a direction in which they would rather not have gone.

Meanwhile, there's a new resident in Drumcondra, a Clareman come up from Kerry, where he has been pasturing sheep for the past few years. He does not have to raise his voice except when, drowned out by the clamour of television, radio and printing press, he cannot otherwise be heard by the sheep.

In contrast to the shepherd's recollected demeanour is that of the leader of the First Orchestra in the Dáil. He claims descent from the noble Fitz-Geralds, and resides in the more desirable environs of the south city. He's edgy and uneasy lest the score should prove unpopular and the orchestra be dismissed before its time. For this performance – unlike previous ones – he appears urbane, having retrieved his spectacles from a holly bush and donned matching shoes. Hard work, a difficult score and long hours of practice supervised by determined foreign tutors who dole out the orchestra's allowances with exquisite meticulousness, have caused him to chew his fingernails.

The first violinist, from Dun Laoghaire, is a benign family man whose background includes caring work with the Legion of Mary – a strange paradox in view of his promotion of the orchestra's present programme. What particularly puzzles people, especially parents, is what connection family planning ought to have with the single state. The answer, of course, as everyone should know by now, is that today's family has been restructured. Ah! That's it. Simple! There are single parent families, and even lesbian and homosexual families now. The bother is that the Irish Constitution only recognises the "traditional" family, but that is merely another hurdle along the path of social progress.

THE STRATEGY

But what has the contraception debate got to do with abortion and the recent Pro-Life Amendment? Simply this: according to the international blueprint *A Strategy for Women's Liberation* –

> The most effective demands for the abortion campaign are repeal of the abortion laws (anti-abortion laws) free and easily available contraception and voluntary sterilisation.[3]

And according to Dr. Malcolm Potts of the International Planned Parenthood Federation (London), abortion is a necessary back-up service for failed contraception. The fact is that those promoting the change in the 1979 law are aiming at the free availability of contraception to all, regardless of age or marital status. Such a move would keep up the pressure for abortion facilities here, which might be provided in the future, were the people to be persuaded to delete the relevant Article from the Constitution – or better still, scrap the present Constitution entirely.

In 1973, the International Planned Parenthood Federation identified progress with regard to contraception in Ireland, one of its target countries, as being at "The pioneering stage when the public is uninformed about family planning and government policy is unfavourable, if not hostile".[4] It thus set out to organise "voluntary associations" within the country which would "motivate the population to demand social change".[5] One such motivator is the IPPF's Irish branch, the Irish Family Planning Association. Following the IPPF *modus operandi*, people in prominent positions in society, and especially within the civil service and Government ministries, are targeted. Once converted, these people then act as human catalysts in effecting the requisite change in a particular society's *mores*. Having created a market, all that remains is to dispose of the eminently saleable and profitable goods: contraceptives, abortion, sterilisation, and as one writer succinctly put it, "take-away babies".[6]

The activities of the IFPA, along with those of other IPPF affiliates led to Mr. Charles Haughey's 1978 Health (Family Planning) Bill which become the Health (Family Planning) Act 1979 and allowed access to contraception by prescription to married people for *bona fide* family planning. The impetus for that piece of legislation came from the judgment in the McGee case, which came before the Supreme Court on appeal from the High Court in December, 1973. The court ruled in favour of Mrs. McGee's right to import contraceptives for her own use within the privacy of marriage. Mrs. McGee had apparently suffered a stroke prior to that time and argued her need for access to contraception on the grounds that her health would be impaired by further pregnancy. In the event, having won her case, Mrs. McGee subsequently produced another baby, proving that either her health was robust enough to support a pregnancy, or that the contraceptives she had won the right to import didn't work, or were not used — or all of the foregoing. Whatever she proved, the fact was that the law would have to be changed to incorporate the legal precedent. The first breach in the dyke had been made in a country which had banned the importation, sale and advertising of contraceptives under its Criminal Law Amendment Act (1935) and the Censorship of Publications Act (1929). Financial backing for the case had come from the Irish Family Planning Rights Association, an offshoot of the IPPF-financed Fertility Guidance Company (1969), the forebear of the Irish Family Planning Association (1973).

The next step involved setting up outlets for the sale of contraceptives which, because of legal restrictions, had until then been given to clients in return for "donations". The Dublin Well Woman Centre was added to the existing outlets when it was set up in 1978. It was established as an offshoot of the Marie Stopes Clinic in London, another IPPF foundation. Apart from providing contraceptives it was to offer a range of services to women, including referral to abortion clinics in Britain for advice. Ann Connolly, a Trinity College graduate, became director after Nuala Fennell, later Minister for Women's Affairs, refused the job. Miss Connolly was to become the leading popularly-fêted protagonist in the campaign to legalise abortion here which began two years later in 1980, with the launching of the Women's Right to Choose Group and its campaign.

The situation would not have arisen but for the existence of the International Planned Parenthood Federation with its nearby London headquarters and worldwide tentacles. Founded in Bombay in 1952, the IPPF grew from the Planned Parenthood Federation of America set up by Margaret Sanger (1939). She was one of eleven children of a poor Irish emigrant man. Having bettered herself through marriage, remarriage and liaisons, she turned her talents and money to controlling reproduction as the remedy for poverty, which she saw as being perpetuated by inferior genes. Thus she magnanimously directed her campaign at the poor with the aim of discarding the "sows' ears" which she decided would never make "silk purses"[7] (her phrase). Her ultimate aim was to breed "a race of thoroughbreds".[8] The Margaret Sanger Research Bureau helped finance development of contraceptives including the IUD and later the pill. She also believed in compulsory sterilisation for the unfit; "human weeds",[9] she called them. Her organisation developed in the climate of the rising tide of humanism in which abortion came to be the accepted back-up service to failed contraception.

Few realise today that the whole contraception-abortion-sterilisation movement has its roots not in socialist idealism, but in right-wing authoritarianism. Margaret Sanger's successors do not like to be reminded of her links with Hitler's Third Reich, but examples abound. For instance, as editor of the *Birth Control Review* between 1917 and 1938, she published in April 1933 an article by a leading Nazi, Professor Ernst Rudin, entitled "Eugenic Sterilisation: An Urgent Need". He advocated a systematic programme of propaganda towards the medical community, followed by the speedy introduction of sterilisation programmes to prevent "multiplication of bad stock".[10] In the same issue, she published an account by a leading American eugenicist, Paul Popenoe, calling for the sterilisation of ten million Americans, while praising the Germans who were "proceeding towards a policy that will accord with the best thought of eugenicists in all civilised countries." This issue also carried an article by Harry H. Laughlin, author of a model eugenic sterilisation law directly adopted by Adolf Hitler, for which Laughlin was given an honorary MD degree by the University of

94

Heidelberg in 1936.

In a letter dated 19 October, 1939, Margaret Sanger outlined a plan for stopping the growth of the Black community in the United States. She suggested that "three or four coloured ministers, preferably with social service backgrounds, and with engaging personalities"[11] be hired to travel through the South, propagandising for birth control. "The most successful educational approach to the Negro is through a religious appeal," wrote Sanger. "We do not want word to go out that we want to exterminate the Negro population, and the minister is the man who can straighten out that idea if it occurs to any of their more rebellious members."[12] A steering committee from Sanger's group would supervise the project while appearing to give control to hand-picked local Blacks. So successful was Sanger's propaganda campaign that her foundation, the Planned Parenthood Federation of America, even managed to gull the Rev. Martin Luther King, who was presented with the "Margaret Sanger Award in Human Rights".[13]

There can be no doubt that Margaret Sanger's ideas — in particular her expressed contempt for "inferior races", were in line with those of the Nazi eugenicists. Experiments carried out in wartime Germany were consistent with Margaret Sanger's philosophy. The world reeled first in disbelief, then in horror at the realisation of the enormity of the crimes committed in concentration camps against innocent people whose only offence was that of having been identified as socially unacceptable and therefore "unfit" because of race, infirmity, and finally religion. Forty years after those atrocities the world seeks to justify — and on a larger scale now — the operation of the principle of utility; and governments propose abortion as being the most cost-effective means of "treating" the handicapped who would otherwise increase demand on their coffers. The handicapped who slip through the net must not engage in "unprotected" sexual activity. If they do, measures must be taken to dispose of their unfit progeny.

Lest the importance of the position relative to contraception be lost, we offer the memorandum overleaf as an object lesson on IPPF-type thinking. Scare tactics about over-population and rapidly-diminishing natural resources are used to sell the notion that fertility and population growth should be reduced, the methods employed being contraception backed up by abortion. The aim is to reduce the population growth to zero, or as near as possible to zero, to relieve pressure on the apparently scarce utilities. The real reason concerns the preservation of multi-million dollar profits of the multinational Corporations, especially in the Third World, and in "underdeveloped" countries of which Ireland is considered one. Hence the attempts to alter our ethic in order to make way for social change which would otherwise be unacceptable. The problem of obtaining money, badly needed to finance industrialisation, education and infrastructure, is solved by yielding to pressure from the international bankers to provide a more "open", secular, non-judgmental and "pluralist" type environment. Many

Memorandum to Bernard Berelson (President, Population Council) found in "Activities Relevant to the Study of Population Policy of the U.S." 3/11/69 by Frederick S. Jaffe (Vice-president of Planned Parenthood – World Population).

TABLE 1. Examples of Proposed Measures to Reduce U.S. Fertility, by Universality or Selectivity of Impact.

Universal Impact	Selective Impact Depending on Socio-Economic Status		Measures Predicated on Existing Motivation to Prevent Unwanted Pregnancies
Social Constraints	Economic Deterrents/Incentives	Social Controls	
Restructure family: a) Postpone or avoid marriage b) Alter image of ideal family size	Modify tax policies: a) Substantial marriage tax b) Child Tax c) Tax married more than single d) Remove parents tax exemption e) Additional taxes on parents with more than 1 or 2 children in school	Compulsory abortion of out-of-wedlock pregnancies	Payments to encourage sterilization
Compulsory education of children	Reduce/eliminate paid maternity leave or benefits	Compulsory sterilization of all who have two children except for a few who would be allowed three	Payment to encourage contraception
Encourage increased homosexuality	Reduce/eliminate children's or family allowance	Confine childbearing to only a limited number of adults	Payment to encourage abortion
Educate for family limitation	Bonuses for delayed marriage and greater child-spacing	Stock certificate type permits for children	Abortion and sterilization on demand
Fertility control agents in water supply	Pensions for women of 45 with less than N children	Housing Policies: a) Discouragement of private home ownership b) Stop awarding public housing based on family size	Allow certain contraceptives to be distributed non-medically
Encourage women to work	Eliminate Welfare payments after first 2 children		Improve contraceptive technology
	Chronic Depression		Make contraception truly available and accessible to all
	Require women to work and provide few child care facilities		Improve maternal health care, with family planning a core element
	Limit/eliminate public-financed medical care, scholarships, housing, loans and subsidies to families with more than N children		

96

of our neighbours in Europe have enthusiastically espoused these ideas and are now beginning to regret their position, faced as they are by zero population growth and an ageing citizenry unable to man their industries or support the non-earners in the community. The natural balance in population structure having been artificially altered, the experiment in demographic engineering has produced unexpected results. Given such a scenario the next logical step to redress the balance is euthanasia, and already there are signs of a shift in the traditional philosophy on the issue. Indeed in Europe, the United States and Britain the first shots in the attempt to overcome resistance have already been fired. The tactics are identical to those employed in the contraception/abortion debates, and the number of legal battles involving the "right to die" are as proliferative as mushrooms.

In a country such as ours, with almost 50 per cent of the population under 25 years of age, it is tempting to think that the answers to many of our social problems lie in a lower birth rate. Judging from the experiences of other countries this does not seem to be so. Already there are signs that the Irish birth rate is declining, despite a fall in the average age of marriage.

*   *   *   *   *

As we awaited the results of the Dáil debate on the contraception Bill, we could not help pondering on the statement that:

> The State's absolute power over fertility constitutes the perfect criterion for social organisation pushed to its extreme limits, and is also a necessary pre-condition for the functioning of a utopian society *after the complete elimination of chance and free will of individuals.*[14] (Emphasis mine)

*   *   *   *   *

Whatever about the social changes to be facilitated by Mr. Desmond's legislation, it was considered in financial circles that there were no quick bucks to be made from the Family Planning Bill. "Entrepreneurs who see business opportunities in Barry Desmond's bill better turn their attention to some other pursuit," said *Business and Finance* on 28 February 1985. But Mr. Patrick Moylett (described by the *Sunday Independent* as "condoms king" nearly a year later) evidently thought differently. Anticipating the passage of the Bill, Mr. Moylett had already circulated possible outlets to advertise his goodies.

> What the Frederick Trading Company is doing for the Irish economy . . . We may not have the big name in condoms in Ireland but we try harder . . . When ordering we hope you will afford us equal oppor-

97

tunity, if only for our greater quality, better price and bigger effort for the Irish economy.

It seems that Mr. Moylett's patriotism and dedication were rewarded and suitably recognised. The *Sunday Independent* of 19 January 1986 stated:

Patrick Moylett made his money out of importing Durex condoms into Ireland, following the legalising of contraceptives in this country. He was recently decorated in Britain by the Gay Federation for pioneering condoms for homosexuals which guard against AIDS.

BACK TO THE FUTURE

Whatever else it may have contributed to International Youth Year it should be noted that the Irish Government facilitated the provision of contraceptives to our young people, whom it considered unfit to marry until the age of majority – which, of course, it then adjusted accordingly! Now one can legally vote, marry and use contraceptives all on the same day – one's eighteenth birthday – though not necessarily in that order, of course! The only discrepancy left to be rectified now is the fact that humans become capable of procreation at a much earlier age than 18 years. However, that problem can be managed by extending access to contraceptives (after a couple of years when the public has had time to adapt and the kids have mastered the art of using them following compulsory State-funded sex education in the schools) to under 18-year-olds as in other countries – with or without parental permission. By that time second-level school students at least (and perhaps some primary kids also) will have become used to obtaining them by virtue of having become sexually active.

The first step in the process is to extend the franchise to 18-year-olds. Then comes free access to contraceptives, and finally a statutory prohibition on marriage until the age of majority. Now, while we are not advocating teenage marriage, is it not surprising that the State should encourage teenagers to use contraceptives while simultaneously forbidding marriage? Perhaps marriage could become old-hat in this scenario? And doesn't this state of affairs remarkably mirror the Planned Parenthood Plan reproduced a few pages back?

If we continue on target Ireland will soon have achieved equality with its European and American neighbours with respect to a rising teenage pregnancy rate, an increasing incidence of sexually transmitted disease, an overall falling birth rate, and fewer marriages. "Stable relationships" and one parent "families" will have become the norm – supplanting the family as it has existed for centuries.

We will then have overcome our "provincialism" and achieved our majority as a nation. We will, like our Western counterparts, then have all the time that is left to our civilisation to regret at leisure. For it is a fact that when the bonds that hold a civilisation together are sundered, that civilisation becomes transformed and fragmented. Once fragmented, like broken china, it cannot be reassembled, and so it is discarded and replaced by something else.

NOTES

1. *The Panchatantra*. Translated by Arthur W. Ryder. Jaico Publishing House, Bombay, 1949.
2. *Ibid*.
3. *A Strategy for Women's Liberation* (Pamphlet). Pilot Books, Wellington, New Zealand, 1974. P. 13.
4. Abel-Smith, Brian. *People Without Choice*. International Planned Parenthood Federation, London, 1973. P. 48.
5. *Ibid*., p. 51.
6. Lowry, Mary. See Chapter 15.
7. Drogin, Elasah. *Margaret Sanger: Father Of Modern Society*. CUL Publications, California, USA, 1979.
8. *Ibid*., p. 12.
9. *Ibid*., p. 15.
10. Drogin, Elasah. *Planned Parenthood's Margaret Sanger: Architect of Modern Society*. Human Life Centre, Collegeville, Min., USA. P. 7. Reprint from International Review of Natural Family Planning. Vol. III, No. 2, Summer 1979.
11. *Ibid*., p. 11.
12. *Ibid*.
13. *Intercessors for America* Newsletter. Ohio, USA, 1 May 1981. Vol. 8, No. 5, p. 3.
14. *Population Development Review*. Vol. 4, No. 2, June 1978. P. 316.

CHAPTER 13

Taking Stock

Given the planning that went into the social changes wrought in Ireland over the last five years, and taking into account those on the way in the near future, it is interesting to audit progress so far. A review of the proposals compiled by the Council for the Status of Women as a result of its Forum described earlier shows the following.

With the exception of the decriminalisation of abortion, most of the goals in the Health category have been attained or are well within reach. More women are remaining on at work after marriage for economic reasons because the average salary of any worker, male or female, is simply not sufficient to provide a home and rear children. Indeed, even the combined salaries of spouses are, in many instances, insufficient to allow them even to think of the possibility of begetting children. Those who do, often have to have their children reared by child minders in private creches. We haven't yet reached the Russian model of state baby farming here, but given trade union demands of late it will appear sooner rather than later. These demands, incidently, are for a 24-hour service designed with the aim of ". . . replacing the family institution".[1]

The status of illegitimacy is on the way out, and presumably eventually also, the legitimacy of marriage. For it is a nonsense to assume that the status of a child born out of wedlock but recognised as legitimate, will not impinge on the status, rights, privileges, inheritance, and exclusiveness of a marriage and its legitimate offspring. After all, why should a man or woman want to marry if, five years on, one finds that one's family must now accommodate the hitherto unheard of offspring of one's spouse, who has just appeared on the doorstep to claim from the inheritance due to oneself and one's children? While I have no wish to denigrate the dignity of a person unfortunate enough to have been born outside of marriage, the conundrum remains. If there is no status of illegitimacy, how can there be one of its opposite – legitimacy?

Divorce and changes in the marriage laws are just around the corner. The legal age for marriage may be raised, and it is not beyond the bounds of imagination to suggest that the future may see us holding examinations for those who wish to marry. In fact one politician has suggested just that. Contraceptives, like beer, are readily available to anybody who wants them. The adoption of legitimate children is under discussion. Attempts have been made to include a definition of rape within marriage in the statutory definition of rape. While one cannot condone sexual assault within marriage, given the nature, rights and duties of the marriage contract it is

100

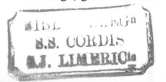

hard to imagine how one would define rape within marriage, unless marriage as such, together with its rights, duties and privacy were to be redefined. Taking a broad look at developments over the last few years it would seem that marriage and the family *are* in fact in the process of redefinition in Ireland.

The laws governing prostitution have come up for discussion also – at least in the media – and models of legislation in operation in other countries have been suggested as a way of protecting prostitutes and controlling the spread of sexually-transmitted disease. Nothing has been said that might suggest that this time-worn profession might be better phased out. Perhaps it may now even be considered one of the caring professions.

As for lesbianism and homosexuality: these are enjoying an unprecedented airing in the media, particularly on RTÉ. On 28 February last we were treated to a radio play featuring a *cri de coeur* from a "bisexual" female. The Gays have it and I don't mean AIDS, though they may have that too for good measure.

The ultimate objective of "freedom of sexual expression" for children, as incorporated in a charter of children's rights, cannot be far off. There are such charters in other countries now, notably Sweden. A ban on corporal punishment in school was the first move on this one. Not a bad thing in itself, the ban on school caning was soon followed by the prohibition of any form of corporal punishment by parents of children in the home. Parents in Sweden can be prosecuted for disciplining their children in the way in which parents have done for centuries. Surely that is the ultimate infringement by the State on the sacred right and duty of parents to rear their children in love and respect? The mind boggles at considering the effect which freedom of sexual expression for children might have. Would incest and deviant sexual practices between adults and children, or children and other children, still cause such controversy, were children to be given such a charter? Food for thought, isn't it?

By far the most significant advances achieved so far have been in the field of education, advances which Mrs. Gemma Hussey proudly noted as being considerable, in her "stand down" interview from the Department of Education given to RTÉ radio during February 1986. The parents' councils planned for both primary and secondary schools have been set up. Teachers have been receiving training in the topic of sex education for about two years now in order to enable the teaching of sex education and lifeskills programmes in our schools. These are well established now, unbeknownst to many parents. The values clarification mechanism upon which these programmes are operated is designed to intervene between the parent and child in order to inhibit the transmission of home norms and values to the child. In this way the . . . "education of children" . . . becomes "the responsibility of society, rather than the individual parents".[2] So much for the recognition of the parents' rights to educate their children!

101

As a mature student at UCD from 1979 to 1981 I felt the impact of the process of values clarification at first hand, in group sessions designed to teach us teachers how to teach ethics to our students, and deal with problems relating to students.

My intense dislike of these sessions, though not of the subject, soon became a joke amongst my colleagues. Whether it was the discomfiture experienced at suddenly having been reduced to student status once more, or the fatigue which followed from trying to defend my values during the group sessions is hard to say: probably both. At any rate I kicked against this goading into group consensus week after week, like a bucking bronco. Being adult and having what I deemed a solid foundation in, and a good apprehension of, medical ethics, I could survive the ever-so-persistent reminders that things were never apparently anything other than coloured grey: and that anyway my thinking was too Thomistic! Somewhere now I hear echoes of that song describing the little boy who eventually succumbed to the notion that flowers are of one colour only! Anyway there were quite a few others of my colleagues who agreed that they found it hard to keep their ends up!

What we were experiencing *de facto* was the Dewey process in action on the ethics field. And our previous training in the use of logic and consistency made our minds do battle with situation ethics. Hence the fatigue we experienced. Values clarification, therefore, was a term well known to at least some graduates as far back as 1980. As we have seen, it is a methodology widely used in our schools now. It is a very useful tool in the hands of those interested in fostering a particular "process" of education free from any given norms, particularly religious norms. As *The Panchatantra* says:

Professor, star-scout, and physician
Find flaws within your home position:
The madman and the snake-charmer know
Points vulnerable in the foe.[3]

As far as the implementation of the schools programme goes, the parents and the home are the "foe".

Much has been said about so-called sexism in education and elsewhere and teachers have, of late, been educated in the methodology for the abolition of role identification in the classroom.

Behind all of this is the battle for the secularisation of all education. The recent attempt to close Carysfort College of Education, the efforts of some teachers to opt out of the teaching of religion in primary schools, and the challenge to the right of Catholic parents to have their children educated at Catholic schools by practising Catholic teachers, as witnessed by the Eileen

Flynn case, are just some of the ways in which the Plan of Action is being operated.

Given our exorbitantly high rates of income tax, not to mention indirect tax, one wonders where the money to finance state-run creches, payment for child rearing at home, free contraceptives for both heterosexuals and gays, sex education programmes, divorce and alimonies, health services for licensed prostitutes, and an education service run exclusively by the state rather than self-sacrificing religious, will come from. Most ordinary workers whose pay is anything above the breadline are already paying 60 per cent of it in income tax. Public services are being cut down or out rather than being expanded, and public servants and others now even fear for their hard-earned and hard-saved pensions. It is not surprising that a country that owes £2,000 million to the International Monetary Fund/World Bank should have had to scuttle its merchant navy along with other assets, and tolerate its government's shameless rifling of children's piggybanks. The fact is now that whatever changes in social mores the IMF dictates, the government will have to facilitate.

NOTES

1. *A Strategy For Women's Liberation* (Pamphlet). Pilot Books, Wellington, New Zealand, 1978; p. 8.
2. *Ibid.*, p. 22.
3. *The Panchatantra, op. cit.*

CHAPTER 14

Through The Looking Glass

The acceptance of the Pro-Life Amendment by the Irish people, and its incorporation into the Constitution must have seemed like the loss of a war to those who had spent years softening up the Irish conscience towards receptivity to International Planned Parenthood Federation ideology. Things would undoubtedly have been easier for them had the 1979 Health (Family Planning) Act made contraceptives freely available then. However they have not been – nor will they be – deterred from their objectives. The signs are that though they have had the hiccoughs, and have had to change tactics somewhat, they inch on relentlessly. As long as they ". . . have access to senior ministers, senior government officials and leaders of public opinion",[1] they should continue to win friends and influence people. The sheer "hang-on-in-there" ability of some of our present public representatives who have links with the IPPF is an obvious advantage.

All in all, 1985-86 has seen three new milestones along the IPPF way in Ireland. These are the opening of Dr. Andrew Rynne's private clinic in Clane, Co. Kildare; the passing of the new Nurses Act; and the commencement of the In Vitro Fertilisation Programme in St. James's Hospital, Dublin.

Before examining the impact of these events with respect to IPPF influence, let us remind ourselves that it is IPPF policy to encourage contraceptives for all (including under-age children) abortion, sterilisation and IVF. The IPPF encourages and sponsors these programmes until it has persuaded the "natives" through its carefully-groomed puppets, to press their leaders for State sponsorship.

The fact that the tiny village of Clane has become home to Dr. Rynne's latest venture – an 18-bed hospital – is curious. In an age when hospitals outside of the major centres are being closed down by the Minister for Health, on the grounds that they cannot be expected to offer adequate medical care as demanded by 1986 standards, it is odd that anybody should want to establish a hospital of its size anywhere in rural Ireland. It is to be wondered also why anybody requiring surgery would not feel safer in the environs of a large general hospital such as the County Hospital just a few miles up the road at Naas. One is curious, too, about Dr. Rynne's plea of financial modesty in his defence when fined for distributing contraceptives in defiance of the then prevailing law. However, as a member of the Irish Family Planning Association and Past President of the European branch of the IPPF, such action was in accord with the latter's objectives. In its "People Without Choice" document of 1973, published in London, the

IPPF urged that members of its national associations should "operate right up to the edge of what is legal . . ."[2] and that they should be ". . . continually taking the next step in breaking social norms . . ."[3]

Being a private concern, presumably there was venture capital available for Dr. Rynne's clinic. One not unreasonably asks where the capital might have originated, given the doctor's mere country practitioner status. One also asks how such a small private hospital could hope to make ends meet on tonsils, toenails and the odd hernia. The public, particularly those who have to pay directly for their medical care (as well as having to foot the bill for those who don't) have all too often heard Mr. Desmond tell them (when he's not preaching about the evils of smoking) that they are better cared for in big public hospitals. In addition, Mr. Desmond has an avowed dislike for private medicine. One can only guess that Dr. Rynne will be recompensed for his efforts by a high turnover of patients requesting lucrative sterilisation procedures. That would also explain the hullabaloo, led by local people, which preceded the opening of the clinic, on the grounds that the principal surgery proposed for the clinic was to be female sterilisation by tubal ligation.

In fairness to Dr. Rynne and Mr. Desmond we must give them both credit for having done their best to have IPPF policy incorporated into Irish culture, and indeed for their continuing efforts to do so.

During 1985 Mr. Desmond sponsored the Nurses Act. While there were many changes needed – and indeed requested – in relation to the structure, training, practice and control of the Nursing Profession both by the profession and by those with a legitimate interest in it, the arrogation to the Minister of powers hitherto unheard of, such as the power to dismiss the entire governing body, An Bord Altranais, caused shock waves throughout the profession. In addition, the omission of a conscience clause to which to appeal in the event of a wish to dissent from co-operation in procedures considered unethical by any individual nurse, coupled with the notion that the Bord, and not the nurse, would issue directives and exercise discretion in any particular situation incensed the majority of nurses. It looks now as if Mr. Desmond's Act effectively means that from henceforth nurses may have to do the bidding of the Bord over that of their own conscience, or stand aside and let others take their jobs. This dictator-like action in framing legislation so intimately affecting the working lives of the members of such a large profession in a country which the Women's Right to Chose Group claimed to be 97 per cent Catholic, has apparently been accepted without so much as a bleat. "And why?" you ask. "Because the majority of the 97 per cent," I answer, "were afraid to give offence to the 3 per cent who are not of the same fold." Will it be remembered in the future, that logically, the 3 per cent may also have lost the recognition of their right to uphold *their* conscientious decisions? I wonder!

Will members of the Nursing Profession here stand up and support one another or will they succumb like falling skittles? Will the profession in this country ultimately change its colours and, like a disreputable ship, fly a flag of convenience as do its American and European neighbours? If so, then not only will the profession suffer, but so too will its clients. There is ample evidence from other countries, Britain in particular, to show that where the traditional Hippocratic ethic has been abandoned, so too have genuine care and service to the people. One cannot care *for* others, after all, unless and until one first cares *about* them. If the ethic of Irish nurses is to be changed dramatically in the future, their patients can expect a less caring attitude from this caring profession.

It must be assumed that if nurses can be persuaded to facilitate the fitting and dispensing of contraceptives, some of them abortifacient, along with the provision of sterilisation and IVF, then surgical abortion and euthanasia will follow. These are on the horizon, for it will only be a short time before an attempt is made to scrap the present Constitution and, with it, the Pro-Life clause.

The public can also expect to pay more for health services offering sterilisation, IVF, etc., along with counselling for patients and staff emotionally minced by their collective experiences. And what of the taxes subscribed to the State purse? Will Irish citizens, in common with citizens of other countries, be forced to consider withholding taxes which fund procedures and services with which they deeply disagree in conscience? Will Irish society have opened a can of worms which, having escaped, will multiply and then eat those who nurtured them . . . "forcing the victim . . . to assist in its own execution"[4]?

But are we gazing too far into the future? I think not. Contraception and the utilitarian philosophy that accompanies it are well established in Ireland. Sterilisations are being performed surreptitiously, often in places where one would least expect. Abortion, while not known to be offered surgically, is available using various combinations of "the pill". In Vitro Fertilisation (fertilisation which takes place independently of sexual intercourse), has just been commenced in Dublin, with the blessing of the Irish Medical Council, the equivalent of Bord Altranais. The first success was hailed at St. James's Hospital recently.

While those who promote IVF do so no doubt, for humanitarian reasons, in an attempt to bring fulfillment to childless marriages, and the controls they exercise in the process may be strict, the whole concept needs examining.

First, let it be said that IVF – because it involves fertilisation (the union of male seed with female egg cell) being effected in a laboratory dish rather than within the woman's body as the result of natural sexual intercourse – separates procreation from sexuality. Next, the tiny new child who begins to develop from the first moment of fertilisation must be examined for observable defects. In principle, defective embryos are discarded: i.e. the tiny new life is killed, washed down the drain, or, simply left to die. Who, after all, would want to carry a deformed child – especially given the trouble and expense of producing him technologically? Then another attempt, or perhaps several, must be made to achieve another embryo before the new living being can be transplanted into the womb of the infertile woman. Subsequent imperfect embryos suffer the same fate. In some cases several egg cells are removed from the woman and, when fertilised, several embryos are implanted in her womb. In some laboratories facilities are available to store "spare" embryos in refrigerators until needed.

The technique is well established in animal husbandry, and indeed it has been very successful. Farmers refer to the operator as the "AI man". It has had a significant impact both on improving cattle stock and in increasing their numbers with consequent material gain for the farmer. In humans, as in animals, both the male spermatozoa and the female eggs or ova required for the process can be obtained from donors. A woman may therefore bear the child of her husband or partner, or the child of a man unknown to her who has donated his sperm to a sperm bank. In theory the woman could also be host to a child conceived in the laboratory from the egg cell of another woman fertilised by the sperm of yet another unknown man. Such surrogacy may not be unknown in the future. Indeed, legal battles over "ownership" rights of children born as the result of surrogacy have already taken place in other countries. One might ruefully ponder on the ownership rights of the *souls* of these little laboratory-grown human beings.

When applied to humans the scenario gives a remarkable echo of Sanger's desire to "breed a race of thoroughbreds". We are not suggesting that all doctors and scientists, nor any of those working in the field of IVF in this country, are necessarily concerned with the perfection of the stock, far from it; nor are we suggesting that they operate from any but the soundest of motives, or outside of the norms laid down by the Irish Medical Council. However, we do suggest that they may have become so engrossed in science and techology as to have become insensitive to, and detached from, the roots of the gentle art of healing.

For the 97 per cent of the Irish population who profess Catholicism IVF is, to use those now immortal words, "out, out, out", and for the following reasons. Firstly, there is the separation of sexuality and procreation, both of which are intimately bound in nature. Therefore, IVF is unnatural and as such, whether the male seed comes from the husband (AIH) or from a donor (AID) it is forbidden by the teaching authority of the Catholic Church i.e. the Pope and the bishops with him. In addition, the use of donor sperm constitutes adultery. Secondly, the method used to obtain the sperm for the process may involve the man in the practice of masturbation. Lastly, IVF is ruled out because of the danger of losing the embryo even in situations of strict control. Experimentation on living or killed embryos is an outright violation of the Christian duty to avoid killing and to respect the human being.

We cannot claim that the "people of God" are free to assemble at any time to pass judgement on the advances of science in order to facilitate their acceptance by the believing community, for the Church is not, and never can be, a mere democracy. To see it solely in that light is to treat Christ as a politician and to misunderstand the chosen status of the Christian.

Dr. George Henry, master of the Rotunda Hospital, in an interview reported in the *Irish Independent* on 5 March 1986 under the headline "Test Tube Babies: Bishops' Attack is Rejected" stated: "There are procedures involved in the technique of IVF which do involve matters that are not approved by the Roman Catholic Church." It is clear therefore that the latest technological advances in reproductive medicine will exercise the consciences of many nurses and doctors in this country as of now.

So far we are right on target, and not at all backward when compared with other countries that do not have the benefit of our Pro-Life legislation. How's that for *progress*?

As Christians, we cannot condemn others for their deeds unless we wish to be condemned ourselves. We can and we must, however, condemn those deeds which do not accord with our Christian ethics.

NOTES

1. Abel-Smith, Brian, *op. cit.*, p. 48.
2. *Ibid.*, p. 67.
3. *Ibid.*, p. 52.
4. Gehlen, Arnold. *Man in the Age of Technology.* Translated by Patricia Lipscomb. Columbia University Press, New York, 1980.

BIBLIOGRAPHY

Abel-Smith, Brian. *People Without Choice.* International Planned Parenthood Federation, London, 1983.

A Strategy for Women's Liberation (Pamphlet). Pilot Books, Wellington, New Zealand, 1974.

De Marco, Donald. *Abortion in Perspective. The Rose Palace or the Fiery Dragon?* Hayes Publishing Co., Ohio, 1974.

Drogin, Elasah. *Margaret Sanger: Father of Modern Society.* CUL Publications, California, 1979.

Drogin, Elasah. *Planned Parenthood's Margaret Sanger: Architect of Modern Society.* International Review of Family Planning, Vol. III, No. 2, Summer 1979.

Gehlen, Arnold. *Man in the age of Technology.* Translated by Patricia Lipscomb. Columbia University Press, New York, 1980.

Irish Women Speak Out. A Plan of Action from the National Women's Forum. Co-op Books, Dublin, 1981.

Intercessors for America Newsletter, 1 May 1981, Vol. 8, No. 5.

Powell, J. *Abortion: The Silent Holocaust.* Argus Books, Texas, 1981.

The Panchatantra. Translated by Arthur W. Ryder. Jaico Publishing House, Bombay, 1949.

(The decision to include this section was taken well after the book was planned. It seemed so appropriate that it just *had* to go in!)

CHAPTER 15

Facilitation in Action: Take-away Babies with Maynooth Sauce

In the late summer of 1985 I was asked by the Ballintrillick Review *to cover a weekend seminar in Maynooth on New Developments in Human Reproduction. It was organised by the Maynooth Union Summer School for professionals in medicine and biology; law, social science, and politics; ethics and theology.*

As a former midwife, I love babies and have seen the arrival of many. But I am also well aware of the anguish of couples who are unable to have families on their own. I believe it was Malcolm Muggeridge who said it is a much deeper tragedy to be childless, than to have more children than one can conveniently manage.

However, it is as the mother of a child handicapped with Down's syndrome that I have become acutely aware of the humanity of every tiny baby – whether that little person be, in the eyes of the world, perfect or imperfect! What frightens me about the whole process in In Vitro Fertilisation is that as scientific techniques are perfected, God will be overruled as man tries to control the quality of his own stock. Bishop Donal Murray puts it much better than I ever could in his book A Question of Morality.

> *"Part of that control, and this too is the nature of the scientific method, will be a kind of quality control. The embryos, to use the term in the loose sense, which do not measure up will be discarded. The scientist will not regard the production of a deformed or handicapped baby as a successful outcome to the procedure. Again, we have to ask ourselves whether such prior selection of those who will be accorded our welcome and recognition is in harmony with the truth about human dignity. That dignity rests not on the quality of life nor on the excellence of the qualities possessed but simply on being human and on being called by God to share in his love."*

Forty years ago in rural Gloucestershire, to a seven-year-old first communicant, the word "Maynooth" had an aura only slightly less impressive

110

than the word "Rome". But when I eventually came to visit that powerhouse of Irish Catholicism, it was only to hear some of the country's leading divines discussing with other experts the pros and cons of bringing together, in a glass dish, a male sperm and a female ovum – the owners of which might not even be on nodding acquaintance.

It seemed strangely inappropriate that before coffee break on the Saturday morning, we were shown a dish of instruments used for "harvesting" human eggs. These exhibits rested on the same desk that must have supported the lecture notes of Manning, Newman and Ronald Knox.

To one who prefers the old-fashioned method of fertilisation, it seemed incredible that 120 people – doctors, priests, nuns and those involved in infertility counselling in hospitals and women's centres – could listen impassively as Dr. Robert Harrison, Associate Professor of Obstetrics and Gynaecology at Trinity College, Dublin, advocated that "a centrally-funded national centre for in vitro fertilisation" should be set up in Dublin "with its own team and facilities, capable of responding to the IVF demands of fertility clinics throughout the country; either handling the whole process for them, or receiving oocytes recovered elsewhere for fertilisation, growth and embryo transfer."

Incredibly, this learned gathering didn't seem to find it in the least bizarre that a sperm from Spiddal and an egg from Ennis should make a hazardous journey across Ireland to become a new human being in an impersonal petri dish in a Dublin laboratory.

Fr. Enda McDonagh, Professor of Moral Theology at Maynooth, did warn that techniques for producing children as "products" akin to other technical products now existed; he thought these techniques could flourish in the future with unknown implications. "This is one of the most serious questions facing humanity since the arrival of nuclear power," he said.

Fr. McDonagh said he "found it difficult to avoid the conclusion" that from the moment of conception one was dealing with a human being. Rather an *odd* phrase, when you come to think of it! It almost sounds as if it might be objectively more convenient if one *could* avoid such a conclusion. Be that as it may, it was a relief to hear Prof. McDonagh add, "The consequences of this argument rule out experimentation on the foetus, experimentation frequently associated with IVF." As for IVF using the husband's sperm, and the wife's ovum – well, that was something which required "fuller ethical consideration" – according to Fr. McDonagh.

With Baroness Mary Warnock jetting in for Sunday's session, one might have expected to hear Dr. Steptoe as well; but perhaps the diet would have been too rich. However, Dr. Berel Held, Professor of Obstetrics and Gynaecology from the University of Texas, gave us the ins and outs of IVF – but not before we were warmed up with a slide-show of sprawling downtown Houston "designed for the automobile", its space centre and university. This preliminary getting-to-know-you session was so successful

111

in generating a cosy atmosphere, full of medical bonhomie, that the chairman (Dr. Declan Meagher of Holles Street Hospital), congratulating Dr. Held on his talk, said he wished he could have seen his own grand-daughter who lives in Houston included in the slide-show. There then broke out a gentle tide of convivial chortling – the sort of noise made only by gatherings of professional men who have dined well.

Dr. Held's work was similar to that of Dr. Patrick Steptoe (remember Louise Brown, the world's first test-tube baby, in 1978?) and he covered the various ways of achieving what was later described in all seriousness as a "take-home baby". (With crispy noodles and fried rice, perhaps?) Obviously feeling that in a religious foundation he should make a bow in the direction of the spiritual, Dr. Held tried to disarm any misgivings his audience might have about such techniques as surrogacy and womb-leasing by appealing to the authority of Holy Writ.

Up on the screen came hieroglyphics which he said were from the Book of Genesis. "And for those of you whose Hebrew is a bit rusty . . ." (more cordial chucklings) up came another slide, this time in English, from Genesis 16. This revealed how, with Sarah's consent, Abraham impregnated her maidservant Hagar. This, Dr. Held explained, was an early example of surrogacy. Presumably we were meant to conclude that if it was in the Bible it must be OK. His next slide, showing the brochure for an American association for surrogate motherhood, illustrated this use of scriptural authority. The organisation was called "The Hagar Institute".

My companion – a doctor – and I gasped at this blatant misuse of scripture, and waited in vain for one of the many priests in the audience to put Dr. Held right. Surely the whole point of the story is that later, by God's express plan, Sarah's fertility was restored? And Hagar's son Ishmael turned out a "wild ass of a man", while it was through Abraham, Sarah and their son Isaac that God's plan of salvation was put into action.

Following the conference, the *Irish Times* headlined the report by its Medical Correspondent, Dr. David Nowlan, "23,000 Couples In Need of IVF Service". However, Dr. John Bonnar (Professor of Obstetrics and Gynaecology at Trinity College, Dublin) pointed out that the causes of infertility are not static but change with the patterns of disease and sexual behaviour in the society. One of the causes, obstruction of the Fallopian tubes, may happen as result of several factors:

1. Sexually transmitted disease, especially gonorrhoea;
2. Pelvic inflammatory disease which may arise as a result of appendicitis and peritonitis; as a complication of the use of the intrauterine device. Pelvic inflammatory disease may also occur following induced abortion and rarely, following normal pregnancy;
3. Tuberculosis;
4. Tubal ligation, especially where this has been carried out by the

technique of cauterisation where the greater part of the tube is destroyed.

Dr. Bonnar went on to point out that the great majority of cases of tubal obstruction are preventable, but that so far very little effort has been directed into this important area of primary health care. Prof. Bonnar didn't say so, but presumably researchers are so excited about developing new techniques that they pass over the elementary ways of preventing disease.

I felt Prof. Bonnar was rather stating the obvious when he said, "The social implications of altering the natural process of human reproduction have an impact on marriage, the family and on the social, legal and psychological identity of individuals". Would the following scenario, I wonder, indicate unspeakable selfishiness? Or would it be a thoroughly natural reaction?

A husband's baby, by a surrogate mother, regularly wakes the wife, roaring for a feed at 2 a.m. After several night of this, she digs her husband in the ribs and says, "Why don't you feed *your* baby for a change – *Daddy*?"

Question times were always limited, but I do wish someone had asked Prof. Bonnar what exactly he meant by saying, "The important issues in embryo reasearch are not medical or scientific but fundamentally *value issues* which will be determined not by scientific criteria but by how *we as society* view the human embryo" (emphasis mine).

It was left to two philosophers from England – both laymen – to place the question of in-vitro fertilisation-embryo transplant (IVF-ET) in an unequivocally-moral context. Both came from the Linacre Centre in London, a charitable trust whose aim is to clarify and develop a Christian response to the ethical problems arising in clinical practice and bio-medical research. It takes its name from Thomas Linacre, friend of St. Thomas More, physician to Henry VIII, and founder of the Royal College of Physicians of England.

John Finnis, a governor of the Linacre Centre and Fellow and Praelector in Jurisprudence from University College, Oxford, demolished the Warnock Report by simply quoting the words of the Baroness herself:

. . . those (members of the Warnock inquiry) who argued that (research using human embryos) should (be permitted) rested their case on two premises. The first was that the embryo immediately after fertilisation is at such a very primitive stage of life that, although indubitably alive and indubitably in some sense human, it is not as continuous with any human individual who might result if it were implanted as to warrant treatment as a full human being. The second

113

premise was that there are advances in science and medicine that could not be made if this research was prohibited and that these advances would greatly benefit full human beings both now and in the future. The argument in effect amounted to this: in a calculation of harms and benefits the very early embryo need not be counted.

In the light of these last words, said Dr. Finnis, the first premise might more frankly have read, "the early embryo is not as continuous with any human individual who might result if it were implanted as to warrant being counted as a human being in any calculation of human harms and benefits." This, he added, would more adequately have spelled out the force of the first premise, though it would have left unimproved the key argument: the wholly mysterious denial of continuity between the embryo early in its development and the same embryo or foetus or child or peer of the realm later in a process which the Warnock Report itself flatly described as "continuous".

Dr. Finnis then delivered the *coup de grace*: "Remember Edwards after the birth of Louise Brown: 'The last time I saw her, she was just eight cells in a test tube. She was beautiful then, and she's still beautiful now'."

In response to Dr. Finnis, Dr. Luke Gormally, Director of the Linacre Centre, pointed out that in the provision of IVF, medicine was getting more deeply locked into practices whose justification lay not in the shared goal of health, but in the desires of clients – desires which were to be satisfied because the technology existed to meet them, and because rationalisations could be supplied for claiming that no one's rights were thereby infringed.

When I spoke to Dr. Gormally afterwards he said that it you carry this argument to its logical conclusion, then doctors should be in a position to prescribe Porsche cars for patients who suffer from a sense of inferiority at having to drive Mini Metros!

It was a pity that there wasn't more time for questions after the important papers of Drs. Finnis and Gormally. As one (medical) doctor and geneticist remarked to me afterwards, the two Linacre men deserved better questions than the ones they in fact got. One came from Dr. Andrew Rynne of IPPF fame, who was present along with many other familiar anti-Amendment faces. Dr. Rynne seemed to think that Dr. Finnis had said that the people involved in IVF were evil. He thought – dare I say piously? – that such judgements should be reserved to the Almighty. John Finnis pointed out that it is the *act* which is wrong, and no guilt necessarily attaches to the participants.

During a coffee break I asked Dr. Colm O'Herlihy of Holles Street Hospital if the guidelines on IVF were legally binding. "Not at all," he replied; "How could they be? There's nothing illegal about IVF."

How I wish I'd retorted, "Maybe not; but killing a spare embryo would be." I also wish I'd asked if doctors would replace into a super-ovulated mother an embryo that might develop into a handicapped baby.

114

CHAPTER 16

Softly, Softly, Catchee Paddy: The Role of the NUJ

If thou forbear to deliver them that are drawn unto death, and those
that are ready to be slain;
If thou sayest, Behold, we knew it not; doth not he that pondereth the
heart consider it? and he that keepeth thy soul, doth not he know it?
and shall not he render to every man according to his works?
> —Proverbs 24:11, 12.

They are slaves who will not choose
Hatred, scoffing and abuse,
Rather than in silence shrink
From the truth they need must think;
They are slaves who dare not be
In the right with two or three.
> —James Russell Lowell (1819-1891)

The crowded hall was silent as a bearded young Yorkshire Irishman
approached the platform, removed a jar from a black tubular case, and held
it up for his fellow journalists to see. It contained the preserved body of an
aborted baby boy of 12 to 14 weeks gestation.

"The bruised body of this small child," began Tony Flanagan, "is the
most damning of replies to all who in the name of a phony liberty and a
false equality deny the rights of humankind's most vulnerable and most
innocent members."

He was only halfway through this sentence when his voice was drowned
out by yells of hatred and fury. A chorus of boos and footstamping broke
out like a great storm.

The occasion was the 1976 Annual Delegate Meeting of the National
Union of Journalists, the body which represents the vast majority of the
profession in Britain and Ireland. The place was Buxton, a pleasant town
in the Peak District of Derbyshire. The topic under discussion was free
abortion on demand.

The barracking continued unabated. After a while the union President,
Irishwoman Rosaline Kelly, called repeatedly for order – and briefly got it.
"I think we have seen enough of that now," she told Tony Flanagan icily.
Flanagan returned the jar to its case and tried to resume his speech.

115

But the media men and women did not want to hear. They renewed their baying and catcalling, determined to render his words inaudible. Their efforts were rewarded when Ms. Kelly switched off his microphone from her control board.

Years later Flanagan recalled: "Quite when she turned it off I could not be sure, for I was by then so incensed by the thugs' behaviour that I carried on with my speech at the top of my voice."

The mood of the meeting was summed up by one speaker in these words: "A woman's right to choose is fundamental in the fight for equality. The NUJ must campaign through the media for a woman's right to safe legal abortion under the NHS (National Health Service). And a leading feminist freelance journalist, Angela Phillips added: "We need committees at every level of the union to make sure that policies are carried out."[1]

According to the UK Press Gazette – a publication which reports on media affairs – the conference "responded warmly" to another delegate who, describing herself as a Roman Catholic, said her grandmother had died in a backstreet abortion; her mother had lost a job through deciding not to abort an unwanted child (the speaker's brother); and she herself was glad to have had an abortion.[2]

Speakers opposed to the abortion motion went out of their way to dissociate themselves from Tony Flanagan, making it clear they regarded his conduct as reprehensible in the extreme. The general tone of their speeches was one of anxiety about the "divisiveness" of the issue in the union. As Flanagan expressed it later: "None was prepared to demand that the NUJ look more closely at the barbarity it supported."

One delegate from South-east Ireland (a region which later features prominently in this story) told the meeting he was neither in favour of abortion, nor against it. Couldn't they move on to something on which they were all agreed? he asked.

Even before beginning his speech, Flanagan had learned that he would have no allies at the meeting, but would be acting entirely alone. Preliminary approaches had made him painfully aware of the priorities of most "pro-lifers" within the union. A couple of days before the abortion debate, he approached the Treasurer, John Bailey, a fellow Catholic, and told him he intended to make a strong attack on the NUJ's abortion policy if he got a chance to speak. He got no support from Mr. Bailey, or from two other Catholics, "one of them of the kind you'd hear singing 'Faith of our Fathers' with gusto". Both kept their heads well down on the issue, and one later became a member of the union executive.

The reluctance of many professional Catholics to offer more than token resistance to the NUJ's abortion policy was a phenomenon later to be repeated in Ireland. Most seemed unable to grasp the point that by continuing to pay for the implementation of NUJ policy through their subscriptions, they were helping to promote the cause of abortionism throughout

116

these islands.

Not surprisingly, the result of the 1976 abortion debate at Buxton was to entrench abortion on demand irrevocably into the union's plans for Britain – and for Ireland as well. The meeting resolved to instruct the union executive to give active support for a campaign for free abortion on request, and urged all union branches to participate in local and national actions to achieve this "right". Flanagan resigned from the NUJ on grounds of conscience, refusing to allow his subscriptions to be used for promoting such a policy. He saw that journalists are unique among professional people, in that they have the power not merely to support such views, but to help persuade the public to adopt them.

To understand the role of the NUJ in promoting abortionism in these islands, it is necessary to take a brief look at the union structure. NUJ officials, in common with those of other trade unions, are inclined to baffle those inquiring about their organisation, by referring to sets of initials without explaining what these stand for, and without stating clearly where the power actually resides.

The NUJ represents about 90 per cent of the profession in Ireland and Britain. The word "National" in its title refers to Britain, not Ireland. (Irish journalists have never had their own independent trade union or professional organisation). NUJ headquarters are in London, to which subscriptions are sent. In 1983, for example, the Dublin Broadcasting Branch alone forwarded over £IR20,000 to Acorn House, the union's head office in the British capital.[3]

Like most other corporate bodies, the union has various subsidiary committees, and some of these cater exclusively for the Irish membership. The main point to be constantly borne in mind – in order to understand the rest of this chapter – is that the supreme governing body of the NUJ is the *Annual Delegate Meeting* (to which Ireland sends about 40 delegates, roughly 10 per cent of the total.) "It formulates policy, and all other bodies in the union act as its agents in implementing its policies," explains one union document.[4]

The only other body that need concern us here is the National Executive Council. (Note once again that the "National" refers to Britain, although Ireland is represented on it). The NEC is obliged to administer the affairs of the union in accordance with policy determined by the Annual Delegate Meeting.[5]

Some Irish NUJ "spokespersons" attempt to obscure the essential sovereignty of the Annual Delegate Meeting, claiming that Irish members or their delegates can meaningfully "dissociate" themselves from ADM decisions while continuing to pay for their implementation through their subscriptions. The idea that there are two NUJs: a nasty pro-abortion English one and a nice, furry, pro-life Irish one – is entirely false.

After thus briefly explaining as much about the NUJ structure as the reader needs to know, we can now trace the union's role in the campaign to introduce abortion on demand throughout these islands, but with particular reference to Ireland.

Well before the 1976 Annual Delegate Meeting in Buxton, when Tony Flanagan made himself so unpopular with pro- and anti-abortionists alike, many Irish journalists had already been won over to the "right to choose" cause. The previous year, for example, an interesting letter appeared in the union newspaper, the *Journalist*, containing the following passage:

> In Ireland, where sex education is non-existent, the sale and advertising of contraceptives illegal, and divorce impossible, unwanted pregnancies and unwanted children are even more likely than in Britain. It would clearly be preferable if contraception and family planning advice were freely available, thus allowing women to control their fertility and to choose whether or not to have children. *Even then, abortion needs to be available as a last resort, if pregnancy is not to be a penalty.* [Italics mine]

The letter continues:

> The NUJ's support for the Working Women's Charter which includes the calls for contraception and abortion on demand needs to be translated into action – most immediately in Ireland where the changes are needed urgently."[6]

The letter was signed by Mary Anderson, Janet Martin and Marianne Heron of the *Irish Independent* women's page; Deirdre McQuillan, editor of *Woman's Way*; Brian Trench and Jack Holland of *Hibernia*; and by two sub-editors on the *Irish Times*.

By contrast, in the same issue of the *Journalist*, veteran Dublin freelance Hilary Boyle wrote:

> I wonder how many of your writers who are so pro-abortion have actually seen one. I have, and the foetus suffers both fear and agony . . . There is such hypocrisy about these pro-abortionists that I for one feel physically sick."[7]

One of the undeniable successes of the "pro-choice" campaign in the media and elsewhere was the fact that within seven years, Mrs. Boyle was using equally strong language to attack supporters of the Amendment.

The muscle for NUJ policy was provided mainly by the union's powerful "Equality Working Party" of militant feminists. In 1978, believing that abortionism was being pursued with insufficient enthusiasm in some quarters, the Equality Working Party reminded the National Executive

Council of the 1976 resolution by the Annual Delegate Meeting and called on the Executive to send out propaganda material to all branches – including those in Ireland.[8]

Union policy was steadily toughened up. In 1979, reaffirming support for "a woman's right to choose" delegates instructed the Executive to pursue this policy in conjunction with the British National Abortion Campaign. This body has been described by Tony Flanagan as "Britain's most ruthless, extreme, and anti-Christian abortion group". It is still demanding that every woman should have the right to abort her unborn child right up to the moment of birth, and that doctors and nurses who obstruct this "right" should not be allowed to practise in hospitals where abortion is offered under the National Health Service.

That same year, the NUJ played a major role in the defeat of the "Corrie Bill" – an attempt to tighten up the existing law on abortion in Britain. The NUJ's relentless publicity campaign was carried out through the Equality Working Party, using money provided by the subscriptions of Irish members as well as British. In a circular sent to all branches, the Equality Working Party called for the greatest possible participation in the anti-Corrie campaign by NUJ members.

This campaign included a Hyde Park rally, the supply of stickers, leaflets and circulars, the soliciting of funds for the National Abortion Campaign, and the lobbying of the Houses of Parliament. It is impossible to calculate how much of Irish members' money was spent on this project. The one certainty – as any public relations worker will confirm – is that it takes more than peanuts to promote such activities on so large a scale.

After appealing for funds for the National Abortion Campaign (£10 per branch and £5 per individual was suggested) the Equality Working Party circular then exhorted NUJ journalists to act as pro-abortion propagandists. "Although we are calling on your participation in the campaign as trades unionists we would like to remind you that your participation as journalists may do the campaign even more good in the long run. We will shortly be distributing a breakdown of the Bill (from the Campaign Against Corrie) and any information you require either for campaign purposes, or for journalistic purposes can be obtained from the Campaign office or Journalists Against Corrie members . . ."[9]

In case any branch officers might worry about the ethics of turning themselves or their members into pro-abortion hacks, the circular concluded: "We are aware that some members of the union have religious objections to participating in this campaign. We would remind them that NUJ policy is achieved through democratic means and that the majority in favour of current policy is substantial. Branch officers who feel unable, personally, to act on this information should pass it on to members of the branch/chapel who do not have such objections." (A "chapel" is a sub-branch).

119

Those responsible for implementing NUJ policy are evidently so out of touch with ordinary human feelings that they believe objections to slaughtering unborn children are on a par with ritual observances like eating fish on Fridays, or abstaining from pork. One man with "religious" objections to the NUJ's anti-life campaign was the union treasurer John Bailey (a Catholic, as we have already noted). At that year's Annual Delegate Meeting (1979) there was an unsuccessful attempt to unseat Mr. Bailey, for failing to implement this policy. In a puzzling speech in his defence, Mr. Bailey spoke of the pain he felt from the "clash of accountability" between union policy and his moral duty.[10] While accepting Mr. Bailey's sincerity, one cannot help wondering why he wanted so badly to remain an officer in a union which was pursuing so repugnant a policy. During the discussion there were some interesting contributions from Irish delegates. Betty Purcell of Dublin Press and Public Relations Branch said that if the union were to distinguish between political questions and questions of conscience it would be getting into a dangerous area; while Eamonn McCann (Dublin) of *Sunday World* fame, said the union had already taken a stand and it was a simple matter of women's rights concerning their own bodies.[11]

Mr. Bailey survived: and his case is instructive because it was later used to try to persuade Irish "abortion rebels" to remain in the NUJ. The argument went: "If a man of unimpeachable integrity like John Bailey didn't feel it necessary to leave the union over the abortion issue, then why should *you*? See how the NUJ respects conscientious dissent. Democracy carries responsibilities as well as rights: you people, instead of running away, should stay and fight the issue from within." This temptingly plausible argument ignored the fact that there was never even the faintest hope of overturning the NUJ's anti-life policy.

When the Equality Working Party Circular (referred to above) arrived in Ireland, its reception among journalists was mixed. A few greeted it wwith vocal anger and disgust; others disapproved, but less strongly; some – probably quite a small group, but extremely influential – approved wholeheartedly; while the majority appear to have been fairly indifferent. Even those union activists who could broadly be described as "pro-life" tended to see abortion more as a threat to union solidarity than as a moral outrage. Anyway, a large number of journalists, for differing reasons, would have preferred the circular to have remained on the other side of the channel.

The matter was taken up officially by Brendan O'Brien, Secretary of the Dublin Broadcasting Branch, who wrote to the union's London headquarters to ask the General Secretary, Kenneth Ashton for clarification. What, he asked, was NUJ policy on abortion in a country like the Republic of Ireland, where abortion was illegal? Back came a letter stating that the union "would try to encourage a change in the law in the Republic of Ireland, in consultation with the membership involved" in favour of abor-

120

tion on demand.[12] This view was subsequently ratified by the General Purposes Committee of the NUJ's National Executive Council.

In January, 1980, nearly two pages of the union newspaper the *Journalist* were devoted to the crudest form of pro-abortion propaganda. The agenda for the forthcoming Annual Delegate Meeting in Portrush, Co. Antrim, contained resolutions reaffirming the "right" to abortion and calling for the extension of British abortion laws to Northern Ireland.

At this point, three RTE journalists decided they could no longer remain in a union which used their money to promote such a policy. They wrote to the General Secretary Mr. Ashton, stating that they would resign if the anti-life resolution were carried. "The unborn have no union," declared the dissidents. If the only way we can identify with them is by resigning from our own, then so be it."

The three were told that resignation would be a very foolish step, and that they would very probably be "blacked". The Father (chairman) of the Newsroom Chapel (sub-branch), Derek Davis informed one of them that he, too regarded abortion as murder, but that the way to fight it was from within the NUJ. He thought it was a great pity to commit "kamikaze" over the issue. (Presumably he meant "hari-kiri"). These remarks were delivered in a spirit of such joviality that the dissidents never felt any real fear for their livelihoods. Mr. Davis subsequently, in 1984, won a Jacobs Award "for his ability to temper his delivery of the good news as well as the bad . . . for his personality and humour."

Predictably, the anti-life motion was carried overwhelmingly at Portrush, and the three journalists tendered their resignations to Eddie Barrett, the popular and highly competent chairman of the Dublin Broadcasting Branch of the NUJ (in 1984, President of the British-based union). After outlining their reasons for resigning, they wrote: "It has been suggested that the proper course for us to take would be to stay in the NUJ and fight to change the policy from the inside. While there is substantial anti-abortion opinion among NUJ members in Ireland this has, regrettably, carried no weight because of the overwhelming support for abortion among our British colleagues. There is no reason to think that Irish members will ever be able to alter this policy. If one believes, as we do, that the human foetus is a person, then it follow that its destruction is murder. This is an issue that transcends trade union loyalty, and on which there can be no compromise."

The three resignations were shortly followed by several others, including five from the *Limerick Leader*, and then four more from the radio sub-editorial section of the RTÉ Newsroom. The most notorious "abortion rebel" was Billy Quirke of Enniscorthy in Co. Wexford, whose case we will examine in detail below.

This minor revolt received a fair degree of media coverage. One interesting reaction was that of John Healy, writing in the *Western Journal*: "It is of course a basic issue and for a profession or craft which lives by the doctrine of the public's right to know and freedom of information I am more than interested to know how professional newsmen and newswomen can so readily deny the most basic right of all – the right to life"[13] (a strange contrast to his attitude three years later in *The Irish Times*. when Mr. Healy castigated pro-lifers for indulging in "halo politics").

The "Civis" Column in the Carlow *Nationalist*, after predicting that the NUJ's abortion problem would not be easily swept under the mat, highlighted the futility of trying to fight the union's anti-life policy from within. "To get this 'democratic decision' changed," said Civis, "would be about as easy as enlisting the Ayatollah in the CIA."[14]

The dilemma of the professional journalist with qualms about the NUJ's aggressive advocacy of abortion was illustrated perfectly in a letter to *Hibernia*. It was written by Mary Leland of Cork,[15] in response to the NUJ militant Mary Holland,[16] who had called on women who had had abortions to sign a letter declaring that they had done so – following the example of some wealthy and influential Frenchwomen. Ms. Leland stated: ". . . in a way I feel almost ashamed that I cannot be as confidently assertive about the right to choose abortion as are both my friends and my colleagues . . . I feel that when the NUJ pronounces on matters of quasi political faith and morals it inhibits the positive duty of its members to report without bias or without reflecting their own prejudice."

Around this time the dissidents joined the Institute of Journalists, a smaller union (also with its headquarters in London) which has no policy on abortion and believes that no journalist should be forced to support policies that he or she finds professionally or morally offensive. Tony Flanagan, who had blazed the trail four years earlier, wrote to dozens of Irish journalists, pointing out that the ambition of the NUJ pro-abortionists was the establishment of British-style abortion clinics in Ireland's major cities "and to achieve this they plan to work steadily and covertly on the Irish people's resistance to abortion." His letter added: "You, because of your ability to weaken that resistance through what you write and broadcast, are important to the NUJ plotters." Flanagan maintained that the union's attack on the unborn had been of immense benefit to "Britain's lucrative abortion industry" as it incited journalists to distort the truth about abortion. He suggested that the only effective way for media people to fight the anti-life policy was to leave the NUJ.

Tony Flanagan received just one reply to his circular. It came from Father Brian D'Arcy, a Passionist priest from Mount Argus in Dublin whose column "A Little Bit of Religion" enlightens readers of the *Sunday World* each week. "Dear Tony," wrote Father Brian, "Thank you very much indeed for your letter and the information it contained, it is very much appreciated."[17] However, Father D'Arcy still prefers to remain in the NUJ.

By now, tentative moves were being made to have the NUJ declare that the "right to choose" policy did not apply to Ireland (a vain hope, when one recalls that the Annual Delegate Meeting had just voted for the strongest possible campaign in favour of the extension of British abortion laws to the Six Counties – *against* the wishes of the vast majority of the Northern people). In his letter to Father D'Arcy and others, Tony Flanagan had pointed out the hopeless folly of trying to persuade the NUJ to drop or limit its abortion campaign: "Don't kid yourself: abortionism is more deeply rooted in the NUJ than in any other British trade union . . . The minority of Irish votes would be treated with scorn by the English, Scottish and Welsh delegates, dismissed as a feeble Irish joke," he wrote prophetically.

For reasons of union politics, however, the attempt had to be made, in order to deflect the growing threat to the unity of the NUJ. A special delegate conference of the union's 12 branches in the Republic voted 46-17 to ask the National Executive Council not to extend the policy to Ireland (as though it were not already there!) This conference also voted to initiate a campaign to ensure that all references to abortion were deleted from the union's policy at the next Annual Delegate Meeting. How many special delegates – if any – really believed this campaign had any chance of success, it is impossible to tell. Some no doubt felt they had vindicated their pro-life principles and need not worry about whether the British took any notice or not. Another category of delegate – those who regarded union solidarity as of paramount importance, saw the resolution as a necessary exercise for preventing further defections (whatever their own beliefs in regard to abortion might be). The original draft has been made by Cian Ó hEigeartaigh – one of the sharpest minds in the Dublin Broadcasting Branch – who saw clearly the potential of the abortion issue for fragmenting the NUJ in Ireland. Writing in the *Journalist* later that year Mr. Ó hEigeartaigh gave his person view of abortion thus: "I believe all human beings everywhere have the right to control their own fertility and its results. That includes abortion."[18]

It is worth bearing in mind that well over a quarter of all the delegates present at the special Irish conference voted *against* the motion. Taken together with those who – like Cian Ó hEigeartaigh – voted in favour for purely strategic reasons, it is more than likely that they formed a pro-abortion majority. In any event, the dissidents who had already joined the alternative trade union – the Institute of Journalists – regarded the whole exercise as a "snow job" and were not tempted to return to the fold. What mattered to them was that their former union was promoting the killing of unborn children and would obviously continue doing so. From their point of view as trade unionists, it was of comparatively minor importance where the killings might take place; and they were quite certain that there was no hope whatever of persuading British delegates to scrap the policy altogether.

In September, 1980, about two months after this meeting, the Dublin-based Industrial Relations News Service published an article on maternity leave in Ireland. It stated: "Agreements negotiated by the National Union of Journalists in small publishing houses where women journalists frequently hold senior positions are often in fact more generous than in those which exist in larger and more affluent employments. An interesting feature of several maternity leave agreements, recently negotiated by the NUJ, is the termination clause which is included. Under this clause, women whose pregnancies are terminated are entitled to two weeks paid leave of absence."

The article was followed by a table, setting out details of maternity leave agreements in various firms. It included the following entries:

Company	Category of Worker	Conditions of Payment, etc.
Jemma Publications (NUJ)	Journalists	10 weeks paid. Stillbirth or death additional 4 weeks. Miscarriage/Termination – 2 weeks.
Commercial Information Company (NUJ)	Journalists	13 weeks paid after 6 months service. Stillbirth – 4 weeks; Termination – 2 weeks.

Jemma Publications have stated that they had never regarded this clause as conferring any right to paid leave following abortion, and there is no reason to doubt their word. Commercial Information (the publishers of Industrial Relation News) have said they "do not inquire into the circumstances of the loss".

This immensely significant article received little publicity. Its wide dissemination would have shown up the resolution of the Special Delegate Conference on abortion as nothing more than a charade. A surprising number of otherwise well-informed journalists appear to have had no idea what their union was really trying to achieve. For instance Nollaig Ó Gadhra, writing in the *Irish Catholic* in January, 1981, stated: "The NUJ have been quick to assure people that this British-based union . . . does not wish its pro-abortion stand to be advocated in Ireland", without challenging this assertion. To expose the fallacy one has merely to point to Resolution 79 of the previous Annual Delegate Meeting in Portrush which (as readers will recall) advocated the strongest possible campaign in favour of existing British legislation on abortion being extended to *Northern* Ireland.

Union leaders, meanwhile – well aware of the dangers of pushing their "right to choose" policy too brazenly – were fishing in the Republic's waters with considerable skill. The NUJ strategy could best be summed up as "softly, softly, catchee Paddy". Among themselves, they were quite frank about their ultimate intentions. In a letter to the union newspaper, the *Journalist*, the National Organiser for Britain, Ms. Peta Van den Bergh, said she believed that to bring the NUJ's abortion campaign to Ireland would "lose support for getting better jobs and conditions, and in turn lose support for eventually getting a campaign for abortion." Ms. Van den Bergh also maintained that her views on this matter were shared by Eddie Barrett, one of Ireland's leading NUJ members.[19] As we have already noted, Mr. Barrett was eventually elected President of the NUJ. He has been described by the Journalists' Action Group – a caucus of Irish Marxist and feminist NUJ members drawn mainly from the national newspapers and RTÉ – as "a first-class representative, who was willing to take principled stands on unpopular causes, such as women's right to choose abortion."[20]

The woeful attempt by Irish members "to ensure that all references to abortion were deleted from the union's policy" met its predicted fate at the 1981 Annual Delegate Meeting in Norwich, being contemptuously kicked aside by British delegates. The union attitude, as summed up by the *Catholic Standard* was that "the Paddies may yelp as loudly as they please, as long as they keep sending their subscriptions to London". It is worth noting in passing that the *Standard* was one of the very few Irish papers where the NUJ's writ did not run.

Of the speeches on the topic of abortion made at the Norwich Annual Delegate Meeting, two were particularly significant. Mr. Eddie Barrett made plain his belief that abortion was a trade union issue, on which the NUJ should have a view. He said he was convinced that if a ballot were held on the subject, it would reaffirm union policy.[21] The Dublin NUJ Branch chairman, Eamonn McCann, said there was a growing minority in the Republic in favour of the "right to choose". This minority, he added, reflected "an inexorable and unstoppable shift of opinion". The NUJ, said Mr. McCann, had provoked debate where there was none; the NUJ had put the issue on the public agenda in Ireland.[22]

The meeting did not restrict itself to rejecting the proposal to change union policy; it felt bold enough by now to rub Irish "pro-life" noses vigorously in the dirt with the following resolution, No. 234:

"This ADM reaffirms the union's position on abortion as being that of a woman's right to choose.

"This ADM supports the Woman's Right to Choose Campaign.

"ADM pledges its backing for the newly-formed Woman's Right to Choose Group in Ireland. ADM instructs the NEC to support any move to liberalise existing abortion legislation wherever the union has members."[23]

There was one small crumb of comfort: The meeting decided, by 153 votes to 125, not to condemn the National Executive Council for failing to press the union's abortion policy with sufficient vigour.

Resolution 234 remains the policy of the National Union of Journalists. Can there be any doubt that the NUJ's Irish members – be they pro-life, pro-abortion, or merely indifferent – have been subsidising a campaign to encourage the killing of unborn Irish children in the lucrative abortion mills of Britain and (if the Pro-Life Amendment had failed) to set up similar death factories here? Yet one leading Irish NUJ member had the effrontery to state in a letter to the national papers that "nothing could be further from the truth" than that the NUJ supported legalised abortion in Ireland.[24] He also stated that the Resolution had been passed by a "politically motivated minority" within the NUJ. It was in fact carried by 147 votes to 112 by democratically-elected delegates. And this was *after* an eloquent appeal by Cian Ó hEigeartaigh, who said that if the meeting pledged support for the Women's Right to Choose Group in Ireland, it would ensure that the NUJ had no effective future in the Republic. He appears to have considerably over-estimated the strength of "pro-life" sentiments among Irish journalists.

Some union members – probably the most conscientious – become embarrassed and angry when presented with some of the above facts, expressing the view that it is "scurrilous" and "underhand" to point out such things. Yet virtually all of them, if investigating any trade or profession other than their own, would feel duty bound to report on any unsavoury aspects, without fear or favour. One highly-placed journalist – who shall remain anonymous – suggested that union policy was not abortion on demand, but merely the "right to choose". The only possible reply is that anyone unable to grasp the fact that these two concepts are essentially the same, should be in a less exacting profession than journalism.

After the 1981 Annual Delegate Meeting the abortion controversy within the journalistic profession was effectively buried by the media, with one or two interesting exceptions: most of them involving provincial newspapers where the NUJ was not represented. For instance, the *Midland Topic* reported an unprecedented intervention by John Feeney of the Carlow *Nationalist* during a meeting of the Midland Health Board in Tullamore. Mr. Feeney was allowed to address the Board, to defend the NUJ from criticism voiced by Board members. When he stated that Irish members had "dissociated" themselves from the abortion policy, he was reminded by Dr. Rose Kirby O'Hanlon that Irish NUJ members were still paying their fees to union headquarters in London. "Mr. Feeney, in an emotional state, said he could not contradict that," reported the *Topic*.[25]

In Limerick, where there was a strong anti-NUJ presence among journalists, Mr. Billy Kelly, chairman of the Institute of Journalists (Ireland) and editor of the *Limerick Citizen* was castigated by the *Limerick Weekly*

Echo for questioning the motives of those who remained in the NUJ. Mr. Kelly, the former "Father" (chairman) of the NUJ "chapel" at the *Limerick Leader*, left the union at about the same time as the RTÉ dissidents. It is certainly to the credit of the *Echo* that it printed Mr. Kelly's trenchant reply, which is worth quoting in some length.

> Dear Sir, [wrote Mr. Kelly]
>
> There is at least one journalist working with the *Limerick Weekly Echo* who has remained within the pro-abortion National Union of Journalists (NUJ) out of self-interest. I know because he told me.
>
> He told me he abhors abortion but would remain in a union firmly committed to introducing abortion to Ireland because to leave it might mean his career opportunities would be more limited. The journalist has put his career before human life.
>
> Is that the hallmark of an honourable and moral person? The editorial editor in the *Limerick Echo* seems to think so.
>
> That editorial writer was recently severely critical of me over my attack on the only nationwide pro-abortion organisation in Ireland – the NUJ. The writer protested that local journalists were honourable and moral people, and said I knew that. But I don't know that at all.
>
> The writer said I knew that the *Echo* journalists were fighting with all their might to oppose the introduction of abortion to Ireland.
>
> What I do know about some of the *Echo* staff is that they were very free with their talk. They said they were opposed to abortion and objected to their union policy favouring the spread of this murder to Ireland. But when it came to the time for action I did not notice any *Echo* journalists standing up to be counted . . . They are supporting financially an organisation committed to supporting any move to liberalise existing abortion legislation wherever the union has members.
>
> I cannot accept that a journalist could be opposed to abortion in any serious way while helping to finance the NUJ under those circumstances.
>
> Some Limerick journalists found that the NUJ's policy in favour of abortion was repulsive enough for them to leave that union. Other journalists said they would leave the NUJ but did not. And still more made no secret of the fact that they were not at all worried what sort of policy their union had on the matter and they did nothing. The most pathetic group out of the lot were those who said they would act when the time came, but when they were asked to do so they funked it. And there are members of the *Echo* staff in that category.
>
> The editorial writer says the *Echo* journalists have lost respect for

me. I would not rate the respect of at least some of the *Echo* journalists very highly and so to lose that respect means nothing to me.

Yours sincerely
Billy Kelly (Socrates)
Limerick Citizen
13 Thomas Street.[26]

When so little is known, even within the journalistic profession, about the NUJ's abortion campaign throughout these islands, it is not surprising that so few members of the general public are properly informed. One notable exception is Councillor Mick O'Connell, the great Kerry footballer who publicly criticised Irish members of the NUJ at a meeting in Tralee late in 1981.

He was immediately denounced in the *Kerryman* by one Pat Lynch, who described himself as a "Member of Honour" of the National Union of Journalists. In the course of a lengthy letter, Mr. Lynch extolled his own record of service to Ireland during the Emergency; excoriated Councillor O'Connell as a "green-white-and-yella patriot"; and pointed out what a worthy organisation the NUJ must be because an Irish *priest* - forsooth - had been supplied with a union card to enable him to report events on the continent. As for abortion, Mr. Lynch wrote: "We have no part in that reprehensible practice, and we do not intend to have any part in it. To suggest otherwise is, in our view, just as reprehensible as the practice itself."[27] (Which can only mean that Mr. Lynch believes criticism like Councillor O'Connell's - if directed at the NUJ - is just as evil as killing unborn babies).

Councillor O'Connell's dedication to the pro-life cause is motivated not by chauvinism, but by his dedication to mentally handicapped children: the next in line for extermination in countries which accept abortion.[28] He is the father of a young Down's Syndrome boy, whom he has described as "the joy of our life".[29] His answer to Mr. Lynch was therefore a model of Christian forbearance. After quoting from the Equality Working Party circular mentioned earlier in this chapter, Councillor O'Connell wrote: "The people who want to legalise this type of murder have secured the greatest single asset to their campaign, the support of the NUJ. Publicity is the key to any case and we all know the amount of publicity these people are getting. The journalists of Ireland have a grave responsibility in this matter and their power used in defence of the innocents at this time could well be counted as their greatest achievement when it comes to giving an account of their stewardship."

Councillor O'Connell cited the case of the abortion rebel Billy Quirke of Co. Wexford, describing him thus: "Here was a man who was not going to subscribe or be associated (that is, HAVE NO PART) with any union which promoted this abhorrent practice and in doing so risked his very

128

livelihood.''[30]

The case of Billy Quirke is an extreme example of the predicament faced by journalists prepared to pay more than lip-service to their pro-life principles. Before examining in some detail the man and his role in the pro-life struggle, we will bring ourselves as up-to-date as possible with regard to the development of union policy in regard to Ireland.

*   *   *   *   *

The NUJ became – if possible – even more virulently pro-abortion in 1985. That year's ADM in Bristol asserted the "right" of "young women under 16" to obtain abortions without their parents' knowledge or consent, and strongly defended experimentation on human embryos.[31] It also instructed the NEC to send a £100 donation to the British National Abortion Campaign, which is now promoting both these causes. All this – as far as we can ascertain – met with not one squeak of protest from Irish delegates at the time, or from any Branch, chapel, or individual later. It also went unreported in Ireland – except by the *Midland Topic* [32] (where there is a strong chapter of the Institute of Journalists).

We noted earlier the fact that the National Abortion Campaign has demanded that doctors and nurses who fail to co-operate with its anti-life policies should not be allowed practise in hospitals where abortion is offered under the National Health Service.[33] So we come unavoidably to the conclusion that *all* NUJ members – be they British, Irish, pro-abortion, anti-abortion or indifferent – are supporting by their subscriptions a campaign to prevent conscientious Irish doctors, nurses, and midwives from pursuing careers in obstetrics and gynaecology in Britain.

Another interesting development in 1985 concerns the facilities extended to those crossing the water for an "NUJ women's conference" in London. The budget allocation for this gathering was £3,500; and the travel costs of the Irish delegates came to £2,500.[34]

Towards the end of the year, an "Irish advisory delegate conference" in Dublin debated the following resolution: "This conference condemns the attempt by SPUC (the Society for the Protection of Unborn Children) to obstruct and deny women access to information on fertility control and pregnancy counselling and fully supports the Well Woman Centre and Open Line Counselling, who are currently providing this essential service." The most revealing contribution to the debate came from the NUJ President, Ray McGuigan, a sub-editor on the *Evening Herald*. "I have no qualms about the merits of this motion," stated Ray. "But if we pass it, we are going to have splits, and breathe life into the IoJ in this country." Despite Mr. McGuigan's fears of defections, the pro-abortion bandwagon had – as Eamon McCann had predicted in 1981 – become "inexorable and unstoppable" by 1985. The motion was carried by a clear show of hands.[35]

129

The sequel to this development was pathetic. One delegate, with great panache, immediately announced his resignation from the NUJ; but after receiving considerable publicity, and much acclaim in pro-life circles, he quietly withdrew it a few days later. Various groups later went through the now-familiar ritual hand-washing exercise of "dissociating" themselves from the offending motion.

In January 1986 the *Journalist* carried a list of motions for debate at the Annual Delegate Meeting in Sheffield in April. Motion 184 was a somewhat strengthened paraphrase of the one passed at the Irish conference of the previous year. It read as follows: "This ADM condemns the attempt by SPUC to obstruct and deny women access to information on fertility control and pregnancy counselling *which cannot exclude abortion*". (italics mine).

This motion was proposed by the Irish Eastern Branch.

After tracing the history of the NUJ's increasing militancy on the abortion issue, and the pointless politicking of those members who would like this policy changed, one could wish they would heed the advice given by Dr. Julius von Karsteg, the radical German professor, to the naive young Englishman Harry Richmond, who wanted to reform Victorian society:

Your endeavours, my good young man, will lessen like those of the man who employed a spade to uproot a rock. It wants blasting.[36]

1. *UK Press Gazette,* 3 May 1976.
2. *Ibid.*
3. Letter from Treasurer, Dublin Broadcasting Branch, NUJ. January 1984.
4. The Structure of the Union in Ireland. Report of a Joint Committee of the Irish Industrial Council and the Irish Area Council (NUJ). November 1981.
5. *Ibid.*
6. *Journalist*, October 1975.
7. *Ibid.*
8. Annual Report of NUJ Equality Working Party (Anna Coote, Chairperson), Acorn House, 314 Gray's Inn Road, London, WC1X 81 DP.

9. Circular AC 18 (1979/80), NUJ. Address as above.
10. Report of 1979 ADM of NUJ.
11. *Ibid.*
12. Correspondence dated 22 October 1979.
13. Healy's Say, *Western Journal*, April 1980.
14. *Carlow Nationalist*, April 1980.
15. *Hibernia*, 1 May 1980.
16. *Hibernia*, 17 April 1980.
17. Letter from Rev. B. D'Arcy dated 21 July 1980.
18. *Journalist*, December 1980.
19. *Journalist*, 1980.
20. JAG c/o Liberty Hall, Dublin. Letter to members, 1983. In spite of this assertion by some of his supporters, Mr. Barrett later pointed out in an open letter (undated, 1982) to Kevin Moore of Independent Newspapers that he had successfully urged the NEC to declare that the union had no plans to press for the adoption of British abortion legislation in the Republic. This was, however, an empty gesture on the NEC's part, for three reasons: (a) The union's real plans – for abortion on demand – went far beyond existing British law; (b) As previously noted, the NEC has no authority to revoke decisions of ADM; (c) NEC must have been well aware that any such plans – to campaign for the adoption of British legislation – would have been regarded as a breach of Irish sovereignty, and therefore opposed by virtually all Irish members, even the most militant pro-abortionists.

    JAG committee members Patrick Kinsella and Nuala Ní Dhomhnaill voted against a mildly plaintive draft motion before the Republic of Ireland Industrial Council on 19 November 1981 which would have asked the 1982 ADM to "take note" of the problems which the "Right to Choose" policy has caused for the Union in the Republic. Both these JAG members were strong supporters of Mr. Barrett for the Republic of Ireland seat on the NEC.
21. *Catholic Standard*, 4 April 1981.
22. *Journalist*, May 1981.
23. *Ibid.*
24. *Irish Times*, 14 June 1983.
25. *Midland Topic*, 24 September 1981.
26. *Limerick Weekly Echo*, 16 May 1981.
27. *Kerryman*, 11 December 1981.
28. Anyone who thinks this statement is far-fetched should read *Abortion: the Silent Holocaust* by John Powell, pp. 40-57.
29. Letter to writer. 28 December 1981.
30. *Kerryman*, December 1981.
31. *Journalist*, April 1985.
32. *Midland Topic*, 23 April 1985.
33. *Brief History of the National Abortion Campaign.* 1977. Women for Life, 18 Ash Grove, Penge, London SE20 7RD.
34. *Journalist*, December 1985.
35. *Ibid.*
36. *The Adventures of Harry Richmond* by George Meredith. Constable & Co., 1911.

CHAPTER 17

The Case of Billy Quirke

Nor do I think that our literary men would prove as courageous as Solzhenitsyn against a comparable tyranny, or even the mild form of control we already have. The same trendy establishment, which of course abhors Solzhenitsyn, has firm control of the NUJ. Most of us . . . despise and detest our Writers' Union, but will not admit as much, or even resign from it. We all, I fear, can get as drunk as Tvardovsky; but which of us, if the need arose, would find Solzhenitsyn's courage?
—Richard West, writing in *The Spectator*.

But the big courage is the cold-blooded kind, the kind that never lets go even when you're feeling empty inside, and your blood's thin, and there's no kind of fun or profit to be had, and the trouble's not over in an hour or two but lasts for months and years. . . . Billy had it when he trekked solitary from Garungoze to the Limpopo with fever and a broken arm just to show the Portugooses that he wouldn't be downed by them.''
—Peter Pienaar in *Mr. Standfast*, by John Buchan.

An unlikely martyr, Billy Quirke bears little resemblance to the rosary-rattling anti-abortion stereotype so frequently lampooned in *Magill* or *In Dublin*. His best friends would have to admit that he can be as irascible as a rogue elephant, with a long memory to match.

One of his fellow abortion rebels described Billy Quirke as "one of those big Wexford men who, if they get knocked over on the hurling field, just bounce straight up again.'' Nevertheless, to withstand what Billy went through (and is still to a certain extent enduring) one would need more than just native tenacity. It would require a total conviction in the justice of one's cause: in this case, a firm belief in the humanity of the unborn child.

Quirke has been President of both the Adoptive Parents' Association of Ireland, and the Society for the Protection of Unborn Children - Ireland. In the former post, he expressed outspoken views in sympathy with Protestant couples who found themselves prevented from adopting: in the latter he attempted – with only partial success – to oversee the setting up of a strong, properly-structured, grass-roots organisation.

As a reporter, Billy Quirke is one of the investigative school, now becoming rarer in country newspapers. His combative prose style might deceive one into thinking he was inclined to recklessness. But there is a prudent side to Billy's character, and he would certainly have remained in the NUJ if the union's abortion policy had not forced him to resign. Eight months after his resignation, he wrote:

"My decision to leave the National Union of Journalists was not one taken in haste or lightly made. For 25 years I was a loyal member and never once in that period was I out of benefit. My habit was always to pay my subscription in advance.

"Back in 1955 I was the only member of the journalistic staff of The People Newspapers, Wexford, to be a member of a union. The people who then refused to join the NUJ at my invitation, and who refused to join over a period of years, formed part of the noble body of colleagues who, last June, decided to cut off my livelihood without as much as a thought for the future of my wife or children.

"Why, my readers might ask?

"Because I exercised my right under the Constitution of the Republic of Ireland to be a member of the trade union of my choice. I actually resigned from the NUJ and applied for membership of the Institute of Journalists.

"Prior to that I was offered a 'deal' – if I became non-union I would not be 'blacked'. Three people put this obnoxious proposal to me; it was sufficient incentive for a lifelong trade unionist to take them to the High Court."[1]

For some six weeks after his resignation in April 1980 Billy Quirke was treated with courtesy and respect by his former NUJ colleagues. He was told he was "too good a member to lose", and received a letter from the South-East Branch secretary asking him to "reconsider".

Attitudes changed dramatically after Quirke produced his Institute of Journalists membership card.

"Ninety per cent of the journalists with whom I worked ceased speaking to me, and the profound intellectual decree of an NUJ officer at a meeting in Wexford was: 'We'll nut him'."

The behaviour of the Wexford NUJ members was in remarkable contrast to that of their counterparts in RTÉ, who were quite prepared to allow members not only to leave the union on a matter of conscience, but to join the IoJ.

"The decision to 'black' my copy was made early on," wrote Billy, "but the courage to act on it came slowly. Vague messages about my future were passed on to me, and one loud-mouthed individual told the officials and members of Enniscorthy Urban District Council that they would 'take me for every penny I have'."

Billy Quirke informed his colleagues that he had taken a decision of conscience; that the very thought of abortion in their policy was abhorrent to him. He did not want a confrontation, and he appealed to be allowed to conduct his business in his own way and to the satisfaction of his employers.

By an extraordinary paradox, among the Wexford journalists now busily

133

planning either to ruin Quirke or force him back into the NUJ, were some active members of the local branch of the Society for the Protection of Unborn Children – pillars of their Catholic parish.

"The faceless ones finally decided to grasp the nettle," wrote Billy. "I never had formal notice from them that my copy was to be blacked. The calculated plan of these would-be trade unionists was to inform my managing director, and he, in turn, told me.

"I learned from another source that the decisions of 'the boys of Wexford' was unanimous – 'that we will cut off his livelihood for ever, and make an example of him and his family, in the name of the NUJ and in protection of our closed shop'.

"They claimed that I was 'party to' their House Agreement which was completed with management in the previous January. So I was, but they neglected to say that mine was the only dissenting voice.

"Time and again I have told them that the closed shop is unconstitutional in Ireland, and I could never agree to children yet unborn having to accede to their whims and be forced some day, because it may be their wish to pursue a journalistic career, to join the NUJ."[2]

At the first intimation of the NUJ's plan to deprive him of his livelihood, Mr. Quirke contacted the officers of his own union, the Institute of Journalists. Among those he consulted were the President, Chris Underwood, Home Affairs Correspondent of the BBC, and the Deputy General Secretary Jim Paterson (a Gaelic-speaking Scottish Highlander). The IoJ decided without hesitation to give Quirke whatever support was needed in fighting his case through the courts.

Behind the scenes, Billy Quirke was approached by his bishop, the late Dr. Donal Herlihy of Ferns, who assured Billy that if his family were in difficulties because of his action, help could be made available. Billy, who had not always been on entirely cordial terms with all the local clergy, was deeply touched by this offer, but assured Bishop Herlihy that it would not be needed. The bishop – obviously appalled and saddened by the NUJ's move – said as he shook Quirke's hand on parting: "It's a hard, cruel world, Billy."

The Managing Director of People Newspapers, Mr. Austin Channing, had already made it quite clear to Billy that he deplored the NUJ's action, and would continue paying his salary during the dispute. Nevertheless, the course of justice required that a solicitor's letter be sent to Mr. Channing, containing the following passage:

> We are instructed that you are refusing and failing to publish any articles, features, or copy provided by our Client. We have also been instructed that this is as a result of the direct intervention of the National Union of Journalists. As a result of your refusal and failure to so publish our Client is suffering loss and damage and is already suf-

fering a decrease in his earnings and earning capacity.

Your failure to publish or print our Client's work is clearly in breach of your Contract with him and is also a denial and violation of and an unlawful interference with our Client's rights under the Constitution. Further as a result of your continued support and implementation of the NUJ 'blacking policy' in relation to our Client you are guilty of a conspiracy to deny and violate our Client's Constitutional right of freedom of association . . .

Mr. Channing swore an affidavit before the High Court, stating that the company did not agree with the NUJ "blacking" and promising to pay Mr. Quirke's wages for as long as their action against him lasted.

Mr. Quirke sought an injunction restraining the national organiser of the NUJ, Mr. James Eadie, and the Father of the Wexford People Chapel, Mr. Philip Murphy, from interfering with him in his occupation as a journalist. Billy and his friends waited in considerable apprehension in the well of the court, as the judge prepared to issue his decision. If no injunction were forthcoming, Quirke would probably face a choice between total humiliation at the hands of the NUJ, and the loss of his livelihood. His fellow rebels, too, were understandably nervous; if Quirke lost, it could hardly be long before the NUJ moved against them, to enforce its closed shop.

As so often when judgements are being delivered, it was not immediately clear whether the injunction would be granted or not. Mr. Justice McMahon said the action appeared to raise many issues of constitutional law, namely whether a closed shop agreement could be enforced by unions or employers, if that enforcement involved compelling an employee to remain a member of a union of which he did not wish to be a member.

If the statements made by Mr. Quirke were true, said the judge, then his employers were being prevented from permitting him to work in accordance with his contract of employment. That action by Mr. Eadie and Mr. Murphy would in that case amount to imposing a penalty on Mr. Quirke for refusing to abandon his constitutional right not to be a member of the NUJ.

That, said Mr. Justice McMahon, was the question that had to be decided, if the action were to proceed. Until this *had* been decided, the interests of justice required that Mr. Quirke should not be penalised. He granted a seven-day injunction.

Inaudible but fervent sighs of relief went up from Billy Quirke and his supporters. But this was to be more than a mere breathing space. Because of the valuable publicity the court hearing was bound to bring, the tables had been turned, and the NUJ were now in a spot. If they fought the case through and lost in open court, their defeat would be a signal to scores, possibly hundreds, of disaffected but fearful members that it was now safe to resign from the union on conscientious grounds.

At the second hearing a week later, on 31 July 1980, Mr. Eadie and Mr. Murphy undertook to abide by the terms of the injunction until 13 October. Their counsel said "extremely important matters" had been raised by the court order, and they wanted time to consider them maturely.

As Billy Quirke put it: "The injunction meant that the members of the NUJ must, under penalty of imprisonment for contempt of court, accept my copy, and co-operate with me in all respects in relation to my journalistic work. When the three months expired, a lesson had obviously been learned. The NUJ and their named officers failed to enter a defence, and my Counsel were informed that they were prepared to 'settle'."[3]

It was an intelligent move. By failing to enter a defence to Mr. Quirke's allegations, the NUJ avoided a test case on the closed shop. While they delayed out-of-court negotiations, the case remained *sub judice* and could not be commented upon. In November 1980, the *Sunday Tribune* jumped the gun by reporting "Abortion protest journalist wins his case". That indiscretion cost the editor a court apology, costs, and a donation to an NUJ charity.[4]

Mr. Quirke's legal advisers were told that the NUJ was prepared to pay his costs, and to refrain from interfering with his work as a journalist. That wasn't good enough for Billy. He held out for *damages* – not because of vindictiveness or pride, but because he wanted it to be seen that the NUJ were in the wrong in blacking his copy. "My great hope is that there are journalists in the country who have been suffering and who will now have the courage to release themselves from under the yoke of the NUJ," he wrote.[5]

In June 1981 the action was settled. The NUJ paid Mr. Quirke £1,000 damages, as well as his costs. In a letter accompanying the £1,000 cheque, Billy's solicitor wrote:

> The undertaking given by the NUJ was to withdraw its notice to the People Newspapers in regard to the publication of your articles, to refrain from interfering with the publishing or printing of your written words and/or copy, to refrain from interfering with you in your occupation as a Journalist and to refrain from instructing the members of the NUJ not to handle copy submitted by you.

It was an impressive victory. The settlement indicated that Irish law – unlike British – would uphold the rights of the individual conscience in such a case (or at the very least, that the NUJ's legal advisers were strongly inclined to this opinion). An important precedent, one might think, and a reason for justifiable national pride. An Irish worker had successfully challenged a mighty British trade union on a matter of conscience, forcing it to acknowledge his right to earn a living outside its ranks.

If Billy had been a boilermaker, a nuclear physicist, a doctor or an engineer – indeed, if he had been pursuing any trade other than that of journalism – who can doubt that this most newsworthy settlement would have received massive and enthusiastic coverage in the Irish media? Yet the only reference most papers made to the affair was a brief paragraph reporting that the action had been "settled". The only exception was the Catholic press, free of NUJ influence, which gave the facts in full.[6]

It would be quite wrong to conclude from this that any kind of censorship was imposed – or even suggested – by the NUJ. How then, can one explain how the national Press came to ignore the settlement, when the case was no longer *sub judice*? One can hazard a couple of guesses, and I think the answer may be that journalists, like the rest of the human race, tend automatically to filter out from their conscious minds those unpleasant facts which touch them most nearly. Hence, those with editorial decisions to make may have genuinely, and in good faith, decided that the Quirke story was not of great significance.

Another related possibility – less creditable but equally credible – had been previously articulated by John Healy, writing in the *Western Journal*. Discussing not the Quirke case in particular, but the reporting of the abortion controversy as a whole, Healy had speculated: "After all, as a good union man, you don't take the side of the enemy. We may teach young reporters about objectivity and we may enshrine the virtue of objectivity in our code of conduct – but when it comes to the nitty-gritty we all know whose side we are on, or should be on."[7]

The NUJ's Assistant Secretary, Ireland, Mr. Jim Eadie, assured a Co. Sligo correspondent, during the Referendum campaign: "The union does not control, or influence, what appears or does not appear in the media." Highly commendable. Nonetheless, as John Healy observed in the article referred to above: . . . "there are several ways of choking the cat without stuffing creamery butter down his throat, *tuiginn tú*?" Whether deliberately or not, the cat was well and truly choked as far as publicity was concerned. Very few journalists (let alone the general public) are even aware of the outcome of Billy Quirke's action and its possible significance for them personally. A triumph for Billy it certainly was; but by avoiding a decision in open court, the NUJ managed to emerge comparatively unscathed.

With the action over, one might have expected that the journalists of the People Newspapers, Wexford, would have made their peace with Quirke; but this was not to be. There is an unfortunate – but completely understandable – bitterness in a statement made by Billy after the settlement.

Twelve months after my "copy" was "blacked" by my journalistic colleagues in the People Newspapers, Wexford – and I must state that all other staff members and Management deplored this action – I am still very much in seclusion.

As far as I can recollect only two journalists on the staff spoke to

137

me in the last year, and one only fleetingly.

But it is the way I would have it. I have nothing at all in common with the people who attempted to use a trade union issue to "cover up" for the NUJ's shameful abortion policy.

I look at the action they took against me in this way. I am a journalist for almost thirty years. I have a wife and two children to support. My children's sole means of livelihood is my work as a journalist. They depend on me for food, clothing and an education.

My colleagues in the People Newspapers, Wexford, deprived them of these things, or attempted to deprive them, by their action. . . .

The people that would destroy the future of children aged six years and 10 years care little for the unborn, no matter what protestations some of them may make. . . .

I am happy to have received £1,000 damages from the NUJ and that my considerable expenses in this case have also been met by the NUJ. But the money is not important – it is only an approximation of the amount I have paid into the union since I entered journalism.

What is important is that I have, for ever, the right to earn my livelihood and provide for my wife and children, without interference from them.

I would hope that the silly notion of "fighting from within" by some other journalists who detest the NUJ abortion policy would be forgotten and that they would resign from that union. It is the only language they understand. If there was mass exodus the NUJ would soon have a re-think.

But as long as there are milk-and-water Irish men and women who are prepared to put monetary considerations before principle, the abortion lobby will gain in strength. It simply is not possible to believe in the right to life of the unborn baby and still be a member of an organisation which stresses the contrary and has the contrary enshrined in its written policy.[8]

There was more of the same uncompromising pugnacity in an item Billy wrote for the *Journal* – the newspaper of the Institute of Journalists – in 1981.

How is it possible that Irish journalists – some of them priests of the Roman Catholic Church and others who have been set up as "religious correspondents" – can support a trade union that demands killing as a "human right?

I know quite a few Irish priests, and former priests who are members of the NUJ and who have sat quiet as mice through all of this controversy. Isn't it time they showed example and put into practice Pope John Paul's teachings on abortion?

You do not make yourself particularly popular with anyone by expressing such views.

A man who would write so trenchantly about some of the clergy would be unlikely to have much respect for many of our legislators. At meetings of the SPUC Council, Billy was inclined to listen quietly to what other members said, rightly considering that most of them were better informed on the pro-life front than he. However, on one occasion there was a heated argument about whether certain politicians – who afterwards proved to be vehemently anti-Amendment – should be allowed to appear on SPUC platforms. Some argued that it was good for SPUC's image to be associated with such people; others insisted that the politicians in question, having used the radical feminist lobby for their own purposes, were now cynically trying to make sure they didn't lose the "conservative" vote in the process. At this, one Council officer retorted that they were not experienced enough in the ways of politicians to pass that kind of judgment. Billy Quirke then spoke up. "In my line of business I have known quite a lot of politicians over the years," he said. "Most of them were liars and cheats."

The vendetta against Quirke spread way beyond his professional life. When SPUC first set up a committee in Ireland, the most strenuous efforts were made to prevent him becoming President. A whispering campaign got under way, and there were personal approaches to committee members – always on a "mind you, I've said nothing, but . . ." basis. None of the faceless ones – as Billy would no doubt have called them – were willing to confront him openly, or to put their allegations in writing; and Quirke was duly elected unanimously.

Since the court hearing, Billy Quirke has earned his living free of interference – apart from one minor disturbance which was settled with a whiff of legal grapeshot. During a dispute at the parent company, Independent Newspapers, he was informed that his items would no longer be accepted because he was not an NUJ member.

The chairperson of the Institute of Journalists, Valerie Cox (author of the Handicapped for the Amendment chapter in this book) quickly sounded the alarm. Expressing the "disgust" of her members on learning of this new blacking of Mr. Quirke's work, she issued this statement:

> Our union, the Institute of Journalists, has been through this particular tiresome exercise before. On that occasion we were thoroughly vindicated. Legally and morally, Mr. Quirke has right on his side, and our union will fight his case through to a successful conclusion.[9]

Irish Institute of Journalists officers were instructed by Head Office to take Senior Counsel's advice, which was to the effect that the NUJ were in contempt of court, and would be in serious trouble if the blacking continued. Solicitors' letters were sent to the NUJ officials concerned, and the blacking was lifted.

Fortunately, the incident received a thorough airing in *Intercom*, the magazine of the Catholic Communications Institute. The Editor, Father Cyprian Candon, OP, after checking the facts and taking advice, decided the story was both newsworthy and non-libellous. *Intercom* is distributed to parish priests throughout the country, and so the clergy, at least, were informed. A lively correspondence ensued, in the course of which Billy Quirke confirmed that the story was true in every detail, and congratulated Fr. Candon for having the courage to publish it.[10]

It was, of course, purely coincidental that immediately after this episode, the Communications Institute received a stiff letter from the NUJ, virtually ordering it to stop running courses for would-be journalists.

We noted in the preceding chapter that the muscle for the NUJ's pro-abortion campaign was provided mainly by the Equality Working Party, whose "facilitating" activities were mainly responsible for the defections of Billy Quirke and his colleagues. So we conclude this chapter by taking a brief look at how the Equality Working Party has developed since then.

Now renamed the Equality Council, this body has the power to enforce its will right through the union structure. Each branch is required to have its own "Equality Officer" – a sort of Thought Policewoman (or more rarely, Policeman). The function of these commissars is to ensure that unorthodox ideas, offending against the concept of equality as understood by the NUJ, do not get into the media: or that if they do, the journalists responsible are suitably disciplined. In the words of Mr. Bernard Levin, the duties of an Equality Officer are "to hunt out and persecute all those who are suspected of the sin of believing that men and women are not in all matters identical". The justification for this inquisition is Clause 10 of the union's Rule 18, which forbids discrimination on grounds of gender, among others.[11]

A large poster, put out by the Equality Council, now hangs in many newspaper and other media offices throughout these islands, wherever the NUJ writ runs. BREAK THE MOULD: CAMPAIGN FOR REAL PEOPLE, it declares, somewhat obscurely. (There is a highly successful British pressure group called the Campaign for Real Ale – CAMRA – which has helped to restore traditional brewing). Among the supporters of the Campaign for Real People – according to the poster – are the Equal Opportunities Commission, the NUJ Race Relations Working Party, the NUJ Lesbian and Gay Group, and the Campaign for Homosexual Equality.

It was because Billy Quirke had an even broader idea of personhood than those who control the NUJ, that he fell foul of the union in the first place.

1. *The Journal*. Institute of Journalists, Bedford Chambers, Covent Garden, London WC2E 8HA. September/October 1981.
2. *Ibid*.

3. *Ibid.*
4. *Ibid.*
5. *Ibid.*
6. *Catholic Standard*, 24 July 1981.
7. *Western Journal*, April 1980.
8. *Catholic Standard. Vide supra.*
9. *Intercom.* The Communications Centre, Booterstown Avenue, Co. Dublin. September 1984.
10. *Intercom*, November 1984.
11. *The Times*, March 1985.

CHAPTER 18

Garret's U-Turn

The Feast of the Holy Innocents, 1980, was marked by a torchlight procession through Dublin city centre by more than 5,000 supporters of the Society for the Protection of Unborn Children. They were addressed in Dame Street by the Lord Mayor, Alderman Fergus O'Brien, Fine Gael TD for Dublin South Central who – according to the *Irish Press* – called for the immediate closure of the abortion referral clinics.

Mr. O'Brien described abortion as the greatest crime being perpetrated today against humanity. The taking of human life was murder, he said, and all the legislation in the world would not change that. "I believe," said the Lord Mayor, "that we should examine the inner city referral clinics which refer young girls across the water for abortions. These should be checked out and the necessary steps taken against them." He wanted the complete closure of two clinics which made direct referrals to Britain.[1]

"It is a very positive referral system," said Mr. O'Brien. "If a girl goes along to one of these two clinics she will be given an address in Britain where she will be able to get an abortion."

In spite of Mr. O'Brien's rousing speech, and similar strong statements from Fianna Fáil spokesmen, the abortion traffic continued to grow during the next five years, and no government took any measures to close the referral centres. The general feeling was that the number of abortions would be reduced only by improving services to the unmarried mother. This point, constantly repeated by the feminist lobby, was difficult to refute without appearing excessively hard-nosed and uncaring. Eventually, even SPUC, for the best possible motives, diffused its focus and became involved in providing homes for unmarried mothers – a function best left to such admirable bodies as Cura and Life, which were specifically set up for that purpose. It must be stressed that such social work – vitally important for its own sake – is not a factor in reducing the numbers of abortions. As Nurse Loretto Browne, SPUC's Leinster Region chairperson, expressed it from the pulpit of the Capuchin Church in Church Street, Dublin, in 1981:

> Abortionism is a social disease. When dealing with any disease, one must first attack the source of infection, before tackling the symptoms.

The main sources of infection in this instance, with their ruthless but apparently effective solution to the problem of an unwanted pregnancy, were the referral clinics. Agitation for their closure, however, is not a pleasant chore when compared with caring for the unmarried mother and her child; and this was one reason why the closure of referral clinics was put on the back boiler for so long. The other reason was the Pro-Life Amendment Campaign.

Various aspects of the Pro-Life Amendment Campaign are dealt with in other chapters of this book and doubtless theses will be written on it for several years to come. Our concern here is with the part played by some politicians – notably Dr. Garret FitzGerald: first, their commitment to it; and then, at greater length, the strategy employed in backing off from that commitment.

The first overt sign that the views expressed by Mr. Fergus O'Brien (and also by Dr. FitzGerald) might not necessarily be shared by all the party's policy makers, came in April 1981, when the Campaign was about to be publicly launched. Fine Gael's vice-president, Ms. Maria Stack, a medical student at University College, Galway, was quoted as saying she supported abortion "on medical grounds".[2] SPUC immediately loosed a heavy barrage. It pointed out that in modern medicine there was no obstetrical problem which could not be solved without recourse to abortion, and remarked that Fine Gael appeared to be in disarray over its attitude to abortion.

Dr. FitzGerald rushed in to repair the damage. He expressed the party's unalterable opposition to abortion and pointed out that the previous year, Young Fine Gael had unanimously proclaimed its recognition of the right to life of the human foetus from the moment of conception.[3] Ms. Stack was reported as saying she had been misquoted. A month after this episode, Renagh Holohan wrote in the *Irish Times* that any woman politician even wanting to open up the issue of abortion for discussion "must be mindful of the dreadful hounding of Miss Maria Stack, the Fine Gael vice-president, who made some very mild remarks on the topic."[4]

Around this time, Dr. FitzGerald wrote in response to lobbying from SPUC: "I can assure you, in response to your inquiry that I personally, and the Fine Gael Party are totally opposed to the legalisation of abortion in any shape or form. I feel that I must make my statement as categoric as that, and I hope it responds to your inquiry." This was followed by a rather tetchy but intriguing postscript, in Dr. FitzGerald's own hand. "Frankly, it is a *non-issue* in this country." Be that as it may, the Fine Gael leader was remarkably quick to endorse the Pro-Life Amendment Campaign when it went public shortly afterwards.

The PLAC was formally launched on 27 April 1981 by thirteen organisations including SPUC. Its first move was to approach the Taoiseach, Mr. Charles Haughey of Fianna Fáil, Dr. FitzGerald of Fine Gael, and Mr. Frank Cluskey of Labour. The first two promised a referendum on a Pro-Life Amendment as soon as possible; while Mr. Cluskey gave no firm commitment, while expressing his opposition to abortion. When Joseph Power reported in the *Irish Independent* on 13 May that Labour were not committed in the same way as the other two parties, he received an angry telephone call from Mr. Barry Desmond, TD – later to become Minister for Health and Social Welfare, and one of the strongest opponents of the Amendment. Mr. Desmond berated Mr. Power and told him he had got it all wrong: Labour were just as supportive of the Amendment as were the other two parties.

With the general election safely over and won by the coalition, the leaders of PLAC became a little apprehensive when the Fine Gael-Labour Joint Programme for Government 1981-86 was published. Although Fine Gael had stated before the election that in government, it would initiate a referendum to guarantee the right to life of the unborn child, there was no mention of this promise in the joint programme. A most courteous letter was sent to the Taoiseach (Dr. FitzGerald) by the chairman of the PLAC, Dr. Julia Vaughan, pointing out that in consequence of this omission "some apprehensions have been voiced within our constituent and supporting organisations". It would therefore be extremely helpful, wrote Dr. Vaughan, "if we could have a brief note from you with which we could reassure our members in regard to government intentions in the matter".

This reassurance was duly forthcoming. "There is no significance whatever in the fact that the commitment is not referred to . . . The Government is unalterably opposed to the legalisation of abortion and is committed to take whatever steps are necessary to ensure that an appropriate Constitutional Amendment is brought forward." Nevertheless, the quarterly *Response* (bulletin of the Irish Branch of the Responsible Society) described the omission as an "ominous sign".[5] The main fear at this stage was that Dr. FitzGerald would fail to call a referendum on the Pro-Life Amendment as a single issue, preferring to delay the matter and lump it in with elements of his "constitutional crusade" such as divorce.

Another general election, occurring early in 1982, gave PLAC an unexpected opportunity to apply more pressure. It asked the party leaders, Dr. FitzGerald, Mr. Haughey and Michael O'Leary of Labour whether, if elected, they would initiate the necessary legislation for a Pro-Life Amendment *as a separate issue in 1982*. The worst fears of the more suspicious (or clear-headed?) were realised when Dr. FitzGerald ignored the "separate issue" part of the question and said he would introduce the Amendment within the lifetime of the next Dáil – any time within five years. Mr. Haughey stated quite plainly that if elected, he would introduce the Amendment as a separate issue. Mr. O'Leary did not bother to reply.

In answer to Dr. FitzGerald, PLAC issued the blandest of statements, urging him "to agree to bring forward this important amendment as a separate issue from his general constitutional review".[6] SPUC – although it was one of the constituent organisations of PLAC – took an independent line, noting "with disappointment and alarm" that the Taoiseach had decided to "put the Amendment . . . on the long finger". It also noted that by contrast, Mr. Haughey had decided to bring in the necessary legislation before the end of 1982; and expressed the view that the pro-life people of Ireland – no matter what their political persuasion – would bear these facts in mind when casting their vote.[7]

The incoming Taoiseach, Mr. Haughey, said in response to a question in the Dáil on 23 March 1982 that the new Fianna Fáil government would bring in the necessary legislation to enable the Referendum to be held that year, as a separate issue.[8] The following month he told PLAC that the Attorney-General was studying the drafting of the proposed Amendment and that the Campaign should submit its views to the Attorney-General.[9] Mr. Haughey also indicated to members of SPUC that he would publish the Bill during the Dáil summer recess, and move it when the Dáil resumed. At this stage it looked as if the Referendum could be held in late 1982 or early 1983.

As for Fine Gael: over the previous months the more militant groups represented on the Executive of PLAC had already become more and more convinced that certain powerfully-placed elements within the party were working to reverse its commitment to the Amendment. Notable among these was a barrister, John McMenamin, a member of the Election Strategy Committee for the June 1981 and February 1982 elections, who was described by the *Sunday Tribune* as a close friend of Anne Connolly (founder member of the Women's Right to Choose Group[10]) and also as a friend of Dr. Garret FitzGerald. Then there was the party's former General Secretary and Director of Elections, Peter Prendergast, who became a patron of the Anti-Amendment Campaign.

There followed a strange episode involving Mrs. Nuala Fennell, a member of the Fine Gael Front Bench, who was quoted in the *Irish Press* as stating in San Francisco that a "sectarian" amendment would not pass the party's Constitutional Review Committee. The report went on to quote her as saying the issue had caused huge splits in all three parties; and that most Irish people would welcome a "Fine Gael solution" with great relief, just as soon as it could be brought about.

Back in Ireland, Mrs. Fennell claimed she had been misquoted, but confirmed the worst fears of SPUC and PLAC by saying she had explained her party's position as welcoming the Amendment in the context of general amendments to the Constitution. "In view of the many constitutional inadequacies I further explained that singling out this one issue and refusing to accept opposition proposals to widen the referendum is regarded by many as a government acting in a sectarian manner."

Her syntax was a bit obscure, but her meaning was clear enough. The Minister for the Gaeltacht, Mr. Padraig Flynn, could not resist accusing Mrs. Fennell of flying a kite, and said this could not have been done without the knowledge of her party leader. He charged Dr. FitzGerald with retracting the promise he had once made to support the Amendment. "The absence of this firm undertaking indicates that in the inner sanctum of Fine

Gael there is a tacit acceptance to provide for a legislative framework which would allow for legalised abortion in certain circumstances . . ."[11]

For this, he was severely chastised by the Deputy Leader of Fine Gael, Mr. Peter Barry, who accused Mr. Flynn of "muck-raking". There was no ambivalence in the Fine Gael attitude to the Referendum. They were waiting for the wording to be announced, and in this they were in step with the Catholic Hierarchy, said Mr. Barry.[12]

However, with the Fine Gael Ard Fheis of 16 and 17 October 1982 came the proof that something odd had indeed been going on. A very cleverly-worded motion appeared from the Pearse Morris Branch in Dublin South, which read: "This party, while affirming its opposition to abortion, does not consider the pro-life constitutional amendment contributes anything to the solution of the problem." Pro-life supporters within Fine Gael were particularly alarmed by this motion because they knew that several motions in favour of the Amendment had been proposed, but had not appeared on the programme.[13]

PLAC, as an organisation, did nothing to combat this development; but SPUC did. Coachloads of SPUC stalwarts braved persistent lashing rain and handed out leaflets to every delegate arriving at the Ard Fheis. These pointed out that when approached by PLAC in May 1981 Dr. FitzGerald had promised the Amendment some days before Mr. Haughey; and that the South Dublin motion would break the solemn commitment given by Dr. FitzGerald and Fine Gael and encourage the abortion campaigners.

The Ard Fheis was marked by a brilliantly sardonic speech from Alice Glenn, TD for Dublin Central, during which live television coverage of such events really proved its value. As Mrs. Glenn congratulated Dr. FitzGerald on having been the first to commit his party to the Amendment, and accused the framers of the South Dublin motion of trying to undermine his leadership, viewers were able to watch his reaction to her words. Dr. FitzGerald's face, as his eyes swivelled from left to right and back again, was that of a schoolboy trying hard to disguise his fear that his teacher – and the whole class – may suspect him of concealing bubble gum in his desk. As Olivia O'Leary wrote in her Dáil sketch in the *Irish Times*, Alice knows there are ways to make a party leader hop like a hen on a hot griddle. Commenting further on this episode, Ms. O'Leary said that standing up to be counted – like both Alice Glenn and the framers of the anti-amendment motion had done – was the only alternative to gombeen politics. "It's a vast improvement on closing your eyes and trusting in Garrett," she concluded.[14]

As SPUC continued its leafletting outside the RDS, intense lobbying went on inside. As a result of this, many delegates stayed behind to vote against the South Dublin motion on the Sunday afternoon, when there would normally have been only a handful of people in the hall.[15] The chairman of the session, Mr. Jim Mitchell, strongly recommended that the motion be rejected – and it was massively voted down. The outcome surely convinced the Fine Gael leadership that there was a strong desire for the Amendment within the party grass roots, and paved the way for the acceptance by Dr. FitzGerald of the wording to be proposed by the Fianna Fáil Government.

Mr. Haughey kept his promise – but just as his Government was falling. He introducing the Bill on November 2 – All Souls' Day – 1982. The Bill was immediately endorsed by Fine Gael which promised that if returned to power, it would introduce the very same measure as Fianna Fáil, and have the Referendum before 31 March 1983. In a letter to PLAC, Dr. FitzGerald declared: "This Referendum will not be delayed by any other consideration. This is an integral part of our programme and will be undertaken by any Government that I may have the responsibility of leading after the next General Election."

So enthusiastic was Dr. FitzGerald about the Amendment that he even maintained that one "couldn't get a better wording", and he had taken legal advice on it before making his commitment. Some of the leaders of the pro-life movement could already hear – in anticipation – the popping of champagne corks. With both the major parties supporting the Amendment, passage through the Dáil seemed assured, and the campaign to get out the vote on Referendum Day should have been easy.

What happened next was an example of Facilitation at its most professional. At some stage in the immediate aftermath of his election victory, either Dr. FitzGerald, his National Handlers, or both, decided that the Amendment so recently unanimously endorsed by the Fine Gael Parliamentary Party, was to be abandoned. The problem was: how to do this without unacceptable loss of face, and without a major rebellion in the Parliamentary party. The only possible answer was to discredit the wording, using all the skills of a brilliant public relations team.

To appreciate how this was attempted, it is necessary to understand a little about how public relations practitioners, government and politicians utilise the media. For example, to test public reaction, a story is fed exclusively to one friendly journalist that the government intends, say, to provide massive extra help for farmers. The journalist concerned gets considerable kudos for being ahead of the posse with this information; his paper publishes it prominently, and the story is followed up by the rest of the media. A variation of this technique is for an individual politician to express him or herself in favour of a particular controversial course of action which the Government would like to take. In either case, having flown the kite, one then gauges the intensity of the resulting flak: if the fire is too hot, the government can dismiss the story as "pure speculation", or dissociate itself gently from the views expressed by the politician. Whether Mr. Padraig Flynn was justified in accusing Mrs. Nuala Fennell of flying a kite, in the episode mentioned earlier in this chapter, we cannot say – because we do not know. In any case, it is a practice commonly used by Fianna Fáil as well as coalition governments. The British Government is always up to this kind of thing in Northern Ireland: which is why Loyalists always feel it necessary to roar so loudly.

In the story we are now unravelling, the evidence is mostly circumstantial (apart from the skullduggery brought to light by Handicapped for the Amendment, which is dealt with in another chapter). But it certainly appears that a whole series of kites and inspired leaks was expertly planned, and carried out with near-perfect timing.

The first reported break in the dyke of Fine Gael solidarity to its unanimous written commitment came on 4 February 1983 – a couple of months after the Government took office. The *Irish Times* reported on that day that at a lecture in Belfast, Mr Maurice Manning had expressed serious reservations about the Amendment. The newspaper said that as many as 15 Fine Gael TDs had doubts about the Referendum. It fell to Conor O'Clery to leak the dissension in Fine Gael ranks, stating that the Government was considering a change in wording. He said the new approach would be aimed at protecting the existing law from challenge in the courts.

The following day, a Sunday, Maurice Manning was interviewed on RTÉ Radio, voicing strong objections to the Amendment. On 8 February, the *Irish Times* reported Monica Barnes as saying she would defy the whip and vote against the Amendment. On 9 February, the debate in the Dáil opened on the enabling Bill for the Referendum. The Minister for Justice, Mr. Michael Noonan tabled the original Fianna Fáil wording for debate, but expressed some doubts about it. He said the purpose of the Amendment was to ensure that abortion would not creep into Irish society unless the Irish people so decided at another referendum. The next day, at a meeting of the Fine Gael Parliamentary Party, the Attorney-General, Mr. Peter Sutherland, denounced the wording as introducing abortion and forbidding certain operations then (as now) legal. After much debate and failure to reach a decision, the discussion was adjourned until the following week.

However, instead of waiting for the next meeting, the Taoiseach proceeded to present the Parliamentary Party with a *fait accompli*. Attending a conference of Young Fine Gael in Galway (where there were many motions on the agenda against the Amendment) Dr. Fitzgerald was reported to have announced a postponement of the Referendum. Objections poured in, and it was immediately denied that he had done any such thing.

The Fine Gael Parliamentary meeting had still not resumed when on 15 February, the Attorney-General Mr. Peter Sutherland went on RTÉ Television's Today Tonight and denounced the wording. This was the culmination of the campaign to discredit the "Fianna Fáil" Amendment – as Government spokesmen called it – and with his groundwork now complete, Dr. FitzGerald now felt strong enough to receive a PLAC delegation to discuss a change in the wording – and then to unveil the wording that he and his advisers had already decided to impose.

But his opponents at the grass roots of Fine Gael, and in the Parliamentary Party, were fighting back. The *Catholic Standard* of 18 February 1983 reported that Dr. FitzGerald's attempt to go back on the promise to bring in the original Amendment – with the agreed wording – by the end of March, had infuriated pro-life supporters throughout the country and led to a split in the Fine Gael Party. The *Standard* understood that at least six Fine Gael TDs would be prepared to vote against moves to change the wording; and Fianna Fáil had been quick to take advantage of the Government's disarray by insisting on the same wording and time-scale. The newspaper said it was strongly believed in pro-life circles that Dr. FitzGerald had planned his strategy on the assumption that Fianna Fáil was about to drop Mr. Charles Haughey as leader; and that the party, weakened and divided by his departure, would be unable to mount any effective counter-attack. "Mr. Haughey's survival, it is believed, has thrown the plans to bury the Amendment into disarray."

About this time the Life Education and Research Network published a comprehensive and combative little book – *Abortion Now*. The man they invited to speak at the launching in the Gresham Hotel was none other than Fergus O'Brien TD, whom we met breathing pro-life fire at the beginning of this chapter. They hoped for another fighting, headline-catching speech which would help publicise their book. But Mr. O'Brien – later Minister of State at the Department of Health and Social Welfare under Mr. Barry Desmond – used the occasion not to promote *Abortion Now* but to appeal for "clarity, enlightenment and Christian charity" over the Amendment. He hoped that both sides would look at the wording in a calm way, bearing in mind that people had a right to agree or disagree with the Amendment.[16]

When the Taoiseach met the PLAC delegation they already had a fairly clear idea of what he had in mind, and rejected it out of hand. On 23 March, Dr. FitzGerald unveiled his wording: "Nothing in this Constitution shall be invoked to invalidate any provisions of the law on the grounds that it prohibits abortion." It was unacceptable mainly because it left the legislators free to bring in abortion at some future date. It was the formula leaked by Conor O'Clery in the *Irish Times* six weeks before. Interestingly, Dr. FitzGerald's friend Bruce Arnold had speculated in the *Irish Independent* on 18 February: "Suppose the Amendment were to read: 'No law shall be declared unconstitutional solely by reason of the fact that it prohibits the intentional and unlawful procurement of a miscarriage'."

The quarterly newsletter *Response* remarked in its issue for the Spring of 1983: "If one studies the sequence of events, the daily leaks and defections rising up to a crescendo where finally Dr. FitzGerald could renege on his commitment, one sees the hand of a master PR man."

The strategy came within a whisker of success. Despite whips, threats of expulsion, and loss of career prospects, eight deputies said they would vote down the Fine Gael Amendment. They were: Michael Begley, Liam Cosgrave, Michael Joe Cosgrave, Joe Doyle, Oliver Flanagan, Alice Glenn,

149

Tom O'Donnell and Godfrey Timmons. These were just enough to bury Garret FitzGerald's new amendment and to pass the original one. Eventually, a Fine Gael solution to a Fine Gael problem was agreed. The eight conscientious objectors would abstain from the vote on the Fine Gael wording, thus ensuring its defeat. The rest of the party would then abstain on the original Amendment, thus ensuring its passage. In the event, the Fine Gael rebels were joined by Labour TDs Michael Bell, Frank McLoughlin, Seán Treacy, Frank Prendergast and John Ryan. Monica Barnes and Alan Shatter of Fine Gael crossed the floor to vote against the original wording.

After various filibusterings in the Seanad, and other delaying tactics, the Bill was signed by the President on 4 June 1983. In spite of two attempts in the courts to postpone the Referendum, and rumours that it might be delayed beyond the autumn, polling day was fixed on 7 July for 7 September 1983.

Two days before the referendum, Dr. FitzGerald made a long-promised address to the nation about his position on the Amendment. He repeated the main arguments of the Anti-Amendment Campaign, referring to the possibility that the measure might actually usher in abortion, the difficulties it would cause for some methods of contraception; and to the women who would possibly die as a result of it. As his trump card, he said it was his Christian duty to urge the people to vote against it.

Here was an amazing irony. The head of government, speaking as a Christian, was appealing to the people to do something he had been unwilling to do himself. He had had the chance to vote against the Bill in the Dáil. But in spite of his belief that the Amendment might "kill women", and might bring in abortion, he had merely abstained.

The authors would like to acknowledge permission to use material contained in *Response*, the quarterly newsletter of the Irish Branch of the Responsible Society. Throughout the Amendment campaign, *Response* provided by far the best-informed coverage and analysis of developments.

1. *Irish Press*, 29 December 1980.
2. *Catholic Standard*, 17 April 1981.
3. *Ibid.*
4. *Irish Times*, 5 June 1981.
5. *Response*, Spring 1982.
6. Pro-Life Amendment Campaign news release, 13 February 1982.
7. Telex (undated) from SPUC to the media.
8. *Response*, Summer 1982.
9. Letter from Mr. Haughey to PLAC, 26 April 1982.

10. *Sunday Tribune*, 9 August 1981.
11. *Catholic Standard*, 1 October 1982.
12. *Ibid.*
13. *Response*, Winter 1982.
14. *Irish Times*, 18 October 1982.
15. *Response*, Winter 1982.
16. *Catholic Standard*, 18 February 1983.

CHAPTER 19

Handicapped for the Amendment

At four o'clock on 25 August 1983 a new organisation calling itself Handicapped for the Amendment was launched at a news conference in Buswell's Hotel, Dublin. Of all the organisations spawned by the Amendment debate, this turned out to be one of the most controversial, and was to lead to the most incredible witch-hunt over the ensuing weeks. Earlier that day, a number of known pro-lifers were seen together at lunch in Buswell's: among them Dr. Norrie Buckley, a general practitioner from Killarney and medical director, Beaufort Centre for Mentally Handicapped Children, and Mick O'Connell, former Kerry footballer from Valentia Island, himself the father of a handicapped child. These people appeared on the platform that afternoon.

The news conference itself was exceptionally well attended by the media, and also by a number of individuals with a very real interest in the handicapped – for they were handicapped themselves. The chairman of Handicapped for the Amendment was Eugene Gath, a 24-year-old UCD graduate in mathematical physics, who was then doing post-graduate work at the Massachusetts Institute of Technology. A thalidomide victim, he was born without legs. The other members of the committee consisted of a mixture of handicapped people, their relatives and their friends. The fact that they were new names – and not the same old faces reconstituted to give yet another organisation to one side or the other – probably accounted for the initial interest in the group.

Then came the bombshell. This was not to be an ordinary Press conference to express allegiance one way or the other. This one had been called to launch "secret Government papers" which had fallen into their hands and which – they claimed – suggested that the Government wanted to leave the door open for the abortion of handicapped babies.

Eugene Gath began his speech by alleging that after giving his solemn promise to the people to bring in the original Amendment by 31 March 1983, the Taoiseach, Dr. FitzGerald, in February seemed to be looking for a way out of his commitment. At this point – according to Mr. Gath – the Attorney-General, Mr. Peter Sutherland, solved Dr. FitzGerald's problem by faulting the wording and suggesting an alternative that would leave the Oireachtas free to bring in abortion at a future date.

Mr. Gath then referred to the leaked documents which he insisted were authentic (a claim initially denied by the Government, but subsequently tacitly endorsed by the Garda harrassment of suspected moles). Government intentions towards the handicapped were anything but pure, according to Mr. Gath. "In his criticism of the original wording in February 1983 the Attorney-General said: 'The proposal would close off the possibility of ever permitting abortion in the case of the anencephalic foetus or in other cases of severely deformed foetuses.' Such thinking is the thin end of the wedge and is a chilling warning to the handicapped," said Mr. Gath.

"Again, in his advice of February, the Attorney-General faulted the Amendment because it would not allow abortion in the case of protection of the health of the mother. This is a ground for abortion so wide that most abortions could be performed under it almost on demand. It is in the light of such thinking that one would view with much cynicism the Taoiseach's present contention that the Amendment is dangerous to the lives of the women of Ireland. One of the factors apparently was because it would not allow for the abortion of the handicapped."

Unfortunately, continued Mr. Gath, the Attorney-General's views did not stop at that. "As late as 11 March, the documents show that the Government was trying to frame an Amendment which would allow abortion in the case of severe handicap: if pursued, this would have written the right to selective abortion of the handicapped into the Constitution. It read: '. . . termination of pregnancy where the foetus is known to be incapable of viable life shall not be unlawful'."

"In any case," asked Mr. Gath, "what *is* 'viable life'? In the long term, none us is viable; we all have to die some day. But whether our span be a few hours or 100 years, no human government has the authority to take away our right to life. To downgrade the worth of the unborn handicapped will in the long run lead to a decline in the value of our handicapped people already born . . . Dr. FitzGerald has repeatedly said that he is unequivocally opposed to abortion. Yet how can he say this when his officials – who must surely be acquainted with his real views on the issue – can draft these proposals for selective abortion? The fact that the elimination of the severely handicapped unborn was mooted not only once but many times is the most serious indictment of Dr. FitzGerald and his Government. No wonder the full details of the wheeling and dealing on the abortion issue were never revealed to the Fine Gael Parliamentary Party. If they had been, then I am sure that the number of deputies crossing the floor to vote for the original Amendment would have been overwhelming. The Fine Gael Party is basically a party with a deep sense of justice and I am sure that they would never have condoned any such ideas on the abortion of the handicapped," said Mr. Gath.

Dr. Norrie Buckley pointed out that when the British Abortion Act became law in 1967, it was seen as a genuine attempt to tidy up the existing illegal abortion traffic. "No one foresaw that in fifteen years, two million unborn babies would have been slaughtered." The six statutory grounds for abortion in Britain included "substantial risk of a child being born abnormal"; and this was the clause under which handicapped babies were being killed. "So it doesn't require a Ph.D in logic to see that the sinister talons of the witch hunt being carried out to kill off handicapped babies across the Channel, have a grip on our country as well," said Dr. Buckley.

"Ongoing developments in medicine enable doctors and technicians to discover abnormal conditions in unborn babies earlier and earlier. While some of these are treated – and we've seen some wonderful surgery done 'in utero' – the majority of babies are aborted. Professor Jerome Lejeune, who discovered the abnormality causing Down's Syndrome (mongolism) said that this was the only time in medicine that a 'cure' is achieved by killing the patient. A classic example of this took place recently when two doctors killed in the womb a child who was found to have Down's Syndrome, without physically damaging the other twin. The doctor stabbed the handicapped child in the heart, while still in the womb, and drew out half his blood. The child died, but was not aborted. Several months later the other twin was born alive, and the dead child's body was delivered with the placenta," said Dr. Buckley. She believed this showed "a frightening elitist mentality".

Dr. Buckley pointed out that those with Down's Syndrome constituted the largest single group of mentally handicapped people in the country. "While their condition affects them all in varying degrees, every single cell in their bodies is abnormal. Thus, they are extremely malformed, or to use the document's terminology, severely deformed . . . To talk of eliminating abnormal members of the human family smacks of master-race selection," she said.

"Don't bury your heads and say it couldn't happen here. It *could* happen here. Just look at the finances. It costs about £100 for an abortion, whereas to keep a handicapped person for life may cost thousands of pounds. In times of economic crisis, monetary statistics like these are spine-chilling," added Dr. Buckley.

After the speeches, copies of the alleged documents were passed round. They made heavy reading, but the journalists present grasped their meaning very quickly. If these documents were indeed genuine then the Government was thinking strangely. It meant that certain government departments were actually discussing the introduction of abortion legislation to allow the killing of unborn handicapped babies. In their rush to have an interview for the tea-time news bulletin, RTÉ almost scrambled the Press conference by setting up ancillary lighting and rounding up the speakers from the official platform.

The evening of 25 August was also to be the great public debate on the Amendment – a Today Tonight special which would, once and for all, clarify the issues involved and enlighten even the most confused member of the electorate. In the days running up to the 25th there were arguments and counter-arguments, negotiations and counter-negotiations, all culminating in the withdrawal of the official PLAC contingent from the debate. Emotions were running high on either side and RTÉ was determined not to have its long-awaited debate scuttled by the pro-lifers who, from a broadcasting point of view, were being decidely awkward. So, the programme makers set to, gathering pro-lifers from the highways and byways in order not to be accused of presenting an unbalanced argument. This played right into the hands of the members of Handicapped for the Amendment, who were only too delighted to accept last-minute invitations to join the audience.

The drama of the debate itself was more than matched by the off-screen antics of the participants. Mrs. Alison Davis, paralysed by polio, one of the H for the A members invited to attend, had great difficulty in gaining admission at the revolving doors. Eventually one of the porters arranged entry for her in her wheelchair. Ms. Valerie Cox, who was accompanying Mrs. Davis, then informed an RTÉ representative in the lobby that there would be another participant arriving in another wheelchair in a few minutes time; and could they please arrange the doors accordingly.

"What? Not *another* wheelchair. We can't have that. Too emotive." The RTÉ person then disappeared into the depths of the building to re-emerge with more manpower. They confronted the H for the A members (all five of them had arrived at that stage) who consisted of two people in wheelchairs, two able-bodied members and the Chairman, Eugene Gath, who has artificial legs and walks with the aid of crutches. It was pointed out, very kindly, that there were just too many handicapped people around. Yes, they knew they had been invited, but that really wasn't the point. RTÉ hadn't realised they would be in *wheelchairs* (What *did* RTÉ expect, one wonders?). The point was further brought home when one of the wheelchair participants discovered that it was impossible to visit the toilet without leaving the doors wide open behind her.

The members of H for the A pressed on, into the hospitality suite, where tea, coffee and nervous wrecks abounded. Various splinter groups were rehearsing their positions: remembering what to say, and – more importantly – what *not* to say. Well-known figures on either side were receiving deputations and others were more cautious, walking up and down and trying to decide if the unknown faces in the groups were Pro or Anti. It was as though all the campaigning of the past weeks had led up to this moment in time, these precious minutes on the air waves, and that the vote itself was only secondary to the real business of broadcasting.

Eugene Gath approached Mr. Jim Kemmy of the Democratic Socialist Party and questioned him regarding his position on the Amendment in general, and on abortion in particular. The unwary Mr. Kemmy, with commendable lack of guile, walked right into the trap, and answered in the affirmative. Yes, he did believe that there should be abortion in the case of the handicapped foetus. Mr. Gath then confronted him with his own position as a thalidomide victim, a fact completely unrecognisable to the casual gaze, as Mr. Gath was standing still and not even using his crutches at the time. He pointed out that if Mr. Kemmy's views had prevailed a quarter of a century previously, he would have been eliminated. Mr. Kemmy was undeniably embarrassed by this encounter. His helpers moved in around him as if from nowhere, blocking further contact: one of them rebuking Mr. Gath for being so discourteous to Mr. Kemmy.

Then the RTÉ people decided to press their point about those in wheelchairs. "We just can't let you all in there. There's not enough seats, for one thing." The H for the A people agreed to leave one wheelchair outside; one of their members could manage very well on a chair, thank you. But RTÉ still wasn't satisfied. Then the bell sounded. All in, everybody. Already alerted by the H for the A members, Father Michael Cleary, a known pro-lifer, took off in the general direction of the studio, red beard bristling, pushing Mrs. Davis's wheelchair before him. Ms. Marion Gilligan was assisted by Mr. Brian Cox, and Alice Glenn and Valerie Cox marshalled Eugene Gath in with them: Father Cleary and Mrs. Glenn muttering threats of a walkout if RTÉ so much as protested.

On arrival in the studio it was patently obvious that RTÉ had removed some of the name tags. There were places for the two able-bodied members only. However, a swift re-organisation of RTÉ's seating arrangements – and name-cards – and there was space for everyone.

The standard of the debate was pathetic. Informed and ill-informed, intellectual and ignoramus mingled and argued and shouted one another down, despite the efforts of presenter John Bowman. There were bitter recriminations from both sides. Prominent gynaecologists Dr. Louis Courtney from Cavan and Dr. George Henry, Master of the Rotunda Hospital in Dublin, argued the survival rate for babies of 24 to 26 weeks. Then Brian Cox, committee member of H for the A, managed to get through the sea of waving hands and attract Mr. Bowman's attention. He wanted to know what Monica Barnes, T.D. (on the Anti-Amendment Panel) had to say about the documents released that afternoon. She dismissed them out of hand. On no, Garret wouldn't dream of doing anything like that. At this point, Ms. Valerie Cox, Secretary of H for the A, produced the documents out of a brief case and, walking across the floor, laid them in front of Mrs. Barnes. "This is an intrusion," yelled an irate John Bowman as he visualised the prospect of his guests walking all over his studio and ruining his TAM ratings. "But it's good television," muttered Frank Prendergast, Labour TD for Limerick East, who was sitting beside Ms. Cox on the Pro-Amendment side of the studio. RTÉ went into a commercial break and Ms. Cox went around handing out copies of the documents to the other panel members who were anxiously trying to get a look at them.

156

A little later, Dr. George Henry argued that lives could be put at risk if the Amendment were carried. He instanced the case of a woman suffering from toxaemia (severe high blood pressure) who might need a Caesarian section at a very early stage. In such a situation the baby would be unlikely to survive. But he wasn't giving his profession half a chance, according to Ms. Cox – who then revealed that she herself had been a patient of Dr. Henry's, and had an almost identical case history to the one he described. And he had managed her situation beautifully, and delivered a fine baby boy. Dr. Henry blushed red with the compliment, and one felt that he had perhaps been a little hard on himself and his profession.

Towards the end of the programme Mr. Bowman took a phone call, which turned out to be a statement from the Government denying the existence of the H for the A documents and stating them to be completely false.

Time caught up with the broadcasters, and the programme ended. The RTÉ people weren't a bit happy with it. They hadn't achieved what they set out to do. Everyone was now totally confused. The switchboard was jammed with calls from irate viewers, happy viewers, viewers anxious to get across their own personal viewpoint. The public debate was over. Everyone went into the hospitality room. Well, most people did. Monica Barnes left the studio close to tears. It happened like this. As the programme ended Brian Cox went over to Mrs. Barnes, said hello and held out his hand to her – all in the finest tradition of wanting to chat over their differences. "Are *you* the man?" she choked, still obviously furious at Mr. Cox's question earlier in the night. "I am," he replied. Mrs. Barnes snorted and exited, thereby missing a great cross-section of chat in the hospitality room. Valerie Cox went around giving out further copies of the infamous documents.

The enlightened Michael D. Higgins, middle-aged frequenter of pop concerts, champion of liberated youth, and scourge of the sanctimonious, refused to accept a copy, with uncharacteristic primness. His young readers in *Hot Press* would have been amazed to see this side of the Senator's personality.

Before the debate there were many "unknowns", but now everyone was sure on which side each person stood. There were little conclaves up and down the room, all eyeing one another. "Pros" kept together, and "Antis" kept together, huddled in their own groups for safety. Handicapped for the Amendment had been well and truly launched.

The group continued to campaign in the days up to the Referendum. The Government moved from a position of denying the existence of the documents, to announcing its intention of launching an investigation into how they came to be leaked – a fact which amused more than one observer.

But it was left at that – a mere threat of investigation.

It was not until the Amendment was safely over that the Gardaí became seriously involved in trying to trace the unknown "mole" who had leaked the documents. On Friday 23 September, a Detective-Garda telephoned Ms. Valerie Cox at her home in Raheny and said they wished to interview her in connection with the documents. She agreed, and they made an appointment for that afternoon. By the time they arrived she had decided to have a solicitor present and explained this to them. That was fine. Another appointment could be made via her solicitor. No problem.

But on that Friday evening Mr. Rory Buckley, pro-life activist and husband of Mrs. Patsy Buckley of SPUC, was arrested at work and held for nearly twenty-four hours under the Offences Against the State Act. His home was searched by plainclothes Gardaí with a search warrant. There was public outcry at his treatment, with politicians calling it a flagrant abuse of the Act. Senator Des Hanafin of Fianna Fáil wrote to the Taoiseach, objecting to "the harrassment which members of the Pro-Life Movement are presently experiencing", and demanding an investigation into the treatment of the Buckleys. SPUC issued a statement condemning the Garda activities. Handicapped for the Amendment issued a Press statement expressing their horror at this witch hunt and suggesting that the Gardaí would be better employed in trying to identify the persons behind the type of thinking that had led to the documents in the first place.

Dick Grogan in the *Irish Times* produced one of the most factual accounts of the affair on 29 September. He suggested that the Government were very worried because the existence of a "mole" might prove dangerous in the future on even more sensitive issues.

Ms. Valerie Cox's solicitor was contacted by the Gardaí and a meeting was arranged between two plain-clothes detectives and herself in the presence of her solicitor. They arrived at her home – this suspected den of iniquity – to be met by four very active children who made them extremely welcome, asking the usual childish questions. Emily, aged five, sat right on the Bangarda's knee and asked her to write out sums for her. Clearly a very different scenario to the Garda visit to the Buckleys' home.

The gist of that interview was that Ms. Cox did not have the information the detective required, but they wanted her to sign a statement. No problem there, you might think. The first statement, written in longhand by the male detective, described Ms. Cox as a "a housewife". She protested that there was no such thing or person as a housewife, and she would prefer to be described as a wife, mother and journalist. The detective re-wrote the statement but got his wording a bit mixed up and referred to her as a "mother and wife". This wouldn't do either, as technically, the reverse order of "wife and mother" would be more proper. He agreed and rewrote the statement. Then Ms. Cox noticed that the detective referred to himself as Detective-Sergeant XYZ, but referred to his female colleague as Detective-Sergeant Bangarda XYZ. When Ms. Cox asked why the need to identify her sex but not his, the Bangarda became very interested and wondered why indeed. The poor detective wondered why he'd ever got himself into this situation and expressed the hope that he would never have to interview Ms. Cox on any subsequent occasion. He then grabbed his hastily-written statement, got Ms. Cox's signature and left.

This was the last contact that Handicapped for the Amendment had with the Gardaí. They did, however, receive a great deal of support from politicians, and got a number of letters congratulating them on their stand in a very difficult situation. Nothing further was ever heard of the Garda investigation.

Three years on, one may make a fairly intelligent guess that the government's real concern was about other possible embarrassing disclosures relating to Dr. FitzGerald's U-turn on the Amendment. (It was not surely without significance that the Department of Justice held off the Garda investigation until after polling day). It would not have impressed the electorate if details of the attempt by the Attorney-General, Mr. Peter Sutherland, to get the churches to accept the new wording, were made public.

Among the leaked documents – although never published by the press – were minutes of a meeting between the Minister for Justice, Mr. Noonan, and the Attorney-General. The papers provide a fascinating insight into Government strategy. They reveal, in particular, that the Government was making the most strenuous efforts behind the scenes to sell its new wording to the Presbyterians, the Methodists, and the Church of Ireland.

Mr. Sutherland's contact with the Methodists was Rev. Desmond Gilliland, a strong opponent of the original proposal for a pro-life Amendment, who appeared on Anti-Amendment platforms alongside hard-line pro-abortion agitators. "Mr. Gilliland was a reasonable man himself, but the Methodist Church was the most difficult church from this point of view," said Mr. Sutherland somewhat mysteriously. He did not explain – at least for the record – exactly what he meant by this.

The minutes also reveal that the Taoiseach regarded what the Protestant Churches thought about the matter as more important than what the Roman Catholic Church might have to say. "The Taoiseach wanted an indication from the Churches (primarily the Protestant Churches) that they would not regard the new wording as offensive."

And another example of the thinking of this advocate of pluralism: "The Taoiseach wanted the Protestant churches consulted first, as there had been such an effort made to try to meet their point of view to the greatest extent possible."

As the official Pro-Life Amendment Campaign spokespeople had to repeat *ad nauseam*, the Amendment issue was not in essence, a religious issue at all. It was the Anti-Amendment Campaign, abetted by the Government, which concentrated on this aspect. But one might have expected that the Government, having decided to play the sectarian card, would have treated the Catholic hierarchy with at least as much consideration as their Protestant fellow-Christians.

The Attorney-General, however, took a very dim view of what he regarded as the intransigence of the late Archbishop Dermot Ryan of Dublin. "As regards the Catholic Church, the AG said he had spoken to the Archbishop of Dublin at some length. The Archbishop had been very conservative in the course of the discussion and had spoken with some emotion. He had a considerable influence in this matter . . ."

One may surely speculate with reasonable certainty that a fly on the wall at this meeting of prelate and lawyer would have heard Dr. Ryan leave Mr. Sutherland in no doubt of his disgust at the way Dr. FitzGerald was reneging on what was, after all, the most solemn and specific promise ever given to the electorate since de Valera's pledge to abolish the oath of allegiance to the British Crown.

APPENDIX I

HANDICAPPED FOR THE AMENDMENT

PRESS RELEASE ON SPEECH TO BE DELIVERED BY MR. EUGENE GATH AT THE PRESS CONFERENCE OF HANDICAPPED FOR THE AMENDMENT.

4 p.m. BUSWELLS HOTEL, 25 AUGUST 1983.

GOVERNMENT WANTED TO LEAVE DOOR OPEN FOR ABORTION OF THE HANDICAPPED – SECRET PAPERS SUGGEST WHY TAOISEACH AND HIS ADVISORS DID A U-TURN ON THE AMENDMENT

Secret Government papers suggest that one of the factors behind the Taoiseach's rejection of the original Pro-Life Amendment wording was to leave open the possibility of legalising the abortion of the handicapped, Mr. Eugene Gath, himself a victim of thalidomide, claimed today.

Mr. Gath, a UCD graduate with artificial limbs and founder member of Handicapped for the Amendment, was speaking at a press conference to an audience of handicapped, their parents and friends. "After giving his solemn promise to the people to bring in the present Amendment by 31 March 1983, the Taoiseach in February seemed to be looking for a way out of his commitment," said Mr. Gath.

"At this point, the Attorney-General solved Dr. FitzGerald's problems by faulting the wording and suggesting an alternative amendment which would leave the Oireachtas free to bring in abortion at a future date.

"At the end of the day, this plan was upset by the courage and integrity of TDs from all three main political parties. Thanks to them, those who voted for it and those who abstained, the original Amendment – initially warmly welcomed by the Taoiseach – will be put to the people on 7 September. For the sake of the unborn handicapped, those who cannot speak for themselves, I hope that the Amendment will be roundly endorsed by the people of Ireland.

"Government intentions towards the Handicapped were anything but pure judging from leaked documents which are authentic. In his criticism of the original wording in February 1983, the Attorney-General said: 'The proposal would close off the possibility of ever permitting abortion in the case of the anencephalic foetus or in other cases of severely deformed foetuses'.[1] Such thinking is the thin edge of the wedge and is a chilling warning to the handicapped," said Mr. Gath.

"Again, in his advice of February, the Attorney-General faulted the Amendment because it would not allow abortion in the case of protection of the health of the mother. This is a ground for abortion so wide that most abortions could be performed under it almost on demand," said Mr. Gath.

"It is in the light of such thinking that one would view with much cynicism the Taoiseach's present contention that the Amendment is dangerous to the lives of the women of Ireland. One of the factors apparently was because it would not allow for the abortion of the handicapped."

"Unfortunately, the Attorney-General's views did not stop at that. As late as 11 March, the documents show that the Government was trying to frame an Amendment which would allow abortion in the case of severe handicap: if pursued, this would have written the right to selective abortion of the handicapped into the Constitution. It read: . . . 'termination of pregnancy where the foetus is known to be

161

incapable of viable life after birth shall not be unlawful'.[2] In any case, what is viable life?'' asked Mr. Gath. ''In the long term none of us is viable; we all have to die some day. But whether our span be a few hours or 100 years, no human government has the authority to take away our right to life,'' said Mr. Gath.

''To downgrade the worth of the unborn handicapped will in the long run lead to a decline in the value of our handicapped people already born. And from there it is not a very long step to a new Auschwitz.

''Dr. FitzGerald has repeatedly said that he is unequivocally opposed to abortion. Yet, how can he say this when his officials, who must surely be acquainted with his real views on the issue, can draft these proposals for selective abortion? The fact that the elimination of the severely handicapped unborn was mooted not only once, but many times is the most serious indictment of Dr. FitzGerald and his Government. No wonder the full details of the wheeling and dealing on the abortion issue were never revealed to the Fine Gael parliamentary party. If they had been, then I am sure that the number of deputies crossing the floor to vote for the original Amendment would have been overwhelming. The Fine Gael party is basically a party with a deep sense of justice and I am sure that they would never have condoned any such ideas on the abortion of the handicapped.

''These papers give an ugly glimpse into what the future could hold for the handicapped people of Ireland. I would like to appeal as earnestly as I can to parents and to all organizations and people caring for the mentally and physically handicapped to make these facts known and to go out and actively support the Amendment by voting 'Yes'. Remember, if you vote 'Yes' then you are supporting our right to life.''

SPEECH TO BE DELIVERED BY DR. N. BUCKLEY

We are here today because of our real concern for those who cannot express their own fears - our handicapped children, both born and unborn.

As parents and friends of handicapped people we have an awesome responsibility to love, care for and educate our children. When necessary we must also defend their right - social, legal and moral - all of which stem from the very right to life itself.

You have heard from Mr. Gath that the Attorney-General said in March, that one reason why he opposed the Amendment was that ''it would close off the possibility of ever permitting abortion . . . in cases of the severely deformed foetus''.

Let's look at those three words and see what they mean. My dictionary has for ''severe'' - *extreme*; for ''deformed'' - *malformed*; and for ''foetus'' - Latin for *little one*.

So, having de-jargonised the phrase, what we are left with is: an extremely malformed little one. Now we have things in their true perspective; by looking at the meaning of a cold, medico-legal phrase we see reality. A baby, different from accepted norms, needing extra care and support.

In Britain, in 1967 when the Bill to legalise abortion was introduced, it was seen as a genuine attempt to ''tidy up'' the existing illegal abortion traffic. No one foresaw that in 15 years two million unborn babies would have been slaughtered.

1. Advice of the Attorney-General, early February 1983.
2. Discussion in Attorney-General's office, 11 March 1983.

Today, as I speak, every three minutes one baby will be dismembered, pickled alive or otherwise torn from his mother's womb. In the United States the figure is 4,000 a day; and world wide, 55 million babies are killed by abortion every year.

The six statutory grounds for abortion, which is carried out up to 28 weeks in Britain include:
1. Risk of injury to physical or mental health of the woman (it is under this ground that abortion on demand is carried out);
2. Risk to physical or mental health of existing children;
3. Substantial risk of a child being born abnormal.

It is this last clause under which handicapped babies are being killed. So it doesn't require a Ph.D. in logic to see that the sinister talons of the witch hunt being carried out to kill off handicapped babies across the Channel, has a grip on our country as well.

Ongoing developments in medicine enable doctors and technicians to discover abnormal conditions in unborn babies earlier and earlier. While some of these are treated, and we've seen some wonderful surgery done "in utero", the majority of babies are aborted.

Prof. Jerome LeJeune, who discovered the abnormality causing Down's Syndrome (mongolism) said that this was the only time in medicine that a "cure" is achieved by killing the patient. A classic example of this took place recently when two doctors killed in the womb a child who was found to have Down's Syndrome, without physically damaging the other twin. The doctor stabbed the handicapped child in the heart, while still in the womb, and drew out half his blood. The child died, but was not aborted. Several months later the other twin was born alive, and the dead child's body was delivered with the placenta.

This is a frightening élitist mentality which says, in effect: "Look, little boy, you just don't measure up to our standards of physical and mental perfection, and so we don't have any room for you in this Brave New World of ours!"

Let's face it: Down's Syndrome people are the single largest group of mental handicapped people in this country. While their condition affects them in varying degrees, every single cell in their bodies is abnormal. Thus, they are extremely malformed – or to use the document's terminology, severely deformed.

One might also pose the question: who has the right to deprive mankind of the literary genius of a spastic like Christy Browne, or Christopher Nolan?

To talk of eliminating abnormal members of the human family smacks of master-race selection.

Fr. John Powell, S.J., in *The Silent Holocaust*, reminds us that in Germany the death camps were not set up for the Jews. They were set up for the unwanted, the crippled, the unproductive, the useless bread-gobblers. They were killed, all of them.

From my heart I urge you all, especially those of you in positions of authority in the care and education of handicapped people, to support in every way their handicapped brothers and sisters as yet unborn.

Don't bury your heads and say it couldn't happen here. It *could* happen here. Just look at the finances. It costs about £100 for an abortion, whereas to keep a handicapped person for life may cost thousands of pounds. In times of economic crisis, monetary statistics like these are spine-chilling.

I would urge you to protect the unborn handicapped by voting "yes" for the Amendment.

163

APPENDIX II

EIGHTH AMENDMENT

MEETING IN ATTORNEY GENERAL'S OFFICE ON 11 MARCH 1983

(1) The Secretary and Mr. Terry met Mr. Quigley in his room at 2.15 p.m. Mr. Quigley had requested the meeting earlier because, he said, the Attorney-General wished to have the revised text of the amendment and to bring it to a meeting with the Taoiseach at 3.15 that afternoon.

(2) Mr. Quigley mentioned that in the preceding few weeks there had been contacts between the Attorney-General and a number of churchmen and gynaecologists. One of the matters that had been emphasised by some of the latter was that of the anencephalic foetus, which had no brain and rarely survived after birth. Now that it was possible to identify such a foetus at a very early stage, knowledge of such a pregnancy proved very traumatic for the expectant mother. The Attorney-General considered that some provision might be possible for such extremely exceptional cases. As regards the form of the revised text, the Attorney-General was in favour of providing for the right to life portion of it by an addition to the existing subsection 2°.

(3) The Secretary said he thought it would be extremely difficult to draft anything in the nature of a final text without clear guidelines but asked if Mr. Quigley had a text which could be considered. Mr. Quigley produced the following text of the second sentence (i.e. the qualification of the right to life of the unborn):
> "however, [in particular] medical treatment including intervention [in pregnancy] required to [preserve] [protect] the life of an expectant mother or termination of pregnancy where the foetus is known [conclusively] to be incapable of viable life after birth shall not be unlawful".

This is draft A attached. However, when the complete text, including the first sentence ["Rights in relation to life shall extend to the life of every unborn person."], the Secretary said that this was something less than a right to life.

(4) The draft was then revised and expressed as an addition to the existing subsection 2° (draft B).

(5) Mr. Quigley wrote a brief commentary on the draft and the Secretary wrote comments on the draft (comments 1-4 on "C" attached: the P.S. was added on 14 March).

(6) The Attorney General then joined the meeting and detailed the contacts he had made with the various churches (he repeated this in greater detail to the Minister at the meeting with him on 14 March). In the discussion the Secretary developed the comments he had made on Mr. Quigley's draft. In particular he explained in detail, at the Attorney-General's request, the advantages he saw attaching to the use of the word "pregnancy". He also explained the reasons for not wanting the revised text to be an addition to the existing subsection 2°. For one thing, subsection 2° could only be a particularisation of subsection 1° and that subsection was confined to the personal rights of the *citizen* whereas we were now seeking to protect a personal right of a non-citizen.

(7) It then emerged that the Taoiseach could not attend the arranged meeting. The Attorney-General tried to contact the Minister without success. He said he would meet the Minister early on the following Monday 14 March and to put him

in the picture as he thought he should now step out of the direct contacts with the churches so that he would be available to give advice to the Government in relation to the final text. He himself would be travelling to London on Monday afternoon for a meeting with the British Attorney-General, Sir Michael Havers, and would not be returning until the morning of 17 March.

21 March 1983.

DRAFT OF 11 MARCH

This draft is intended to cover the exclusion from being unlawful of: (1) Accepted terminations of pregnancy (whether called abortions or not) – removal of cancerous uterus, pregnancy in fallopian tube. (2) Medical treatment for other illnesses of mother, e.g. (a) Cancer other than in uterus; (b) Where appropriate, use of post-coital contraceptives. (3) An anencephalic foetus conclusively diagnosed.

Art. 40.3.2°. Add: ". . . and the life of every unborn person. However, in particular medical treatment, including intervention [in pregnancy] required to [preserve/protect] the life of an expectant mother, or termination of pregnancy where the foetus is known [conclusively] to be incapable of viable life after birth, shall not be unlawful."

DEPARTMENT OF JUSTICE COMMENTS (NOT CLEARED WITH MINISTER) ON MR. QUIGLEY'S DRAFT OF 11 MARCH

(1) We do not think the expression "unborn person" meets the published criticisms of the word "unborn" in the present text. It could raise a major question about the meaning of "person".

(2) We think the word "protect" (in the phrase "to protect the life of the mother") is liable to be interpreted as opening the way to abortion in the interests of the mother's health. We do not agree that the word "protect" can be defended on the basis that it already appears in Article 40.3.2° as, in our view, the context is different.

(3) We have seen no evidence that permission to abort an anencephalic foetus would be generally acceptable.

(4) We appreciate the reason the words "in particular" are put in the draft but we think, precisely for that reason, they would be unlikely to be generally acceptable if their intended significance were appreciated.

P.S. – It is taken for granted that the words "required to [preserve/protect] the life of an expectant mother" are intended to apply to "medical treatment" as well as "intervention". Some modification would seem to be needed to make that clear.

APPENDIX III

EIGHTH AMENDMENT

MEETING WITH ATTORNEY-GENERAL IN MINISTER'S ROOM ON 14 MARCH 1983

(1) The Minister was accompanied by the Secretary and Mr. Terry.

(2) He said he had had contacts with representatives of the various churches in connection with the revised wording. He had not contacted the Jewish Community. He had discussed with the Protestant churches an amendment on the lines of that suggested by the Minister whereas he had sought a reaction to his own proposal (the "confirmatory" proposal) from the Catholic Church.

(3) As regards the Church of Ireland, he had been speaking to Dr. Alan Browne, Zion Road, a member of the Synod. He was a member of a subcommittee of the Standing Committee that had been set up to consider the revised wording, when published. The membership of the subcommittee included the Archbishop of Dublin, Dr. McAdoo. Dr. Browne, who was well disposed, had arranged a meeting on Wednesday 16 March on the basis that the wording would then be available. He had told the Attorney-General that it would be helpful to him and others on the sub-committee if the arguments in favour (from their point of view) of the revised wording should be given. The Taoiseach wanted an indication from the churches (primarily the Protestant churches) that they would not regard the new wording as offensive. The Attorney-General had explained to Dr. Browne that the Minister wanted a private meeting before publication on condition that the other churches were given a similar facility.

(4) As regards the Presbyterian Church, the A.G. had been in contact with the Rev. W. T. McDowell . . . His response to the Minister's wording was generally favourable, especially in relation to the use of "pregnancy" and he thought the revised wording was a substantial improvement. He was expected back in town after 8 p.m. that evening and was leaving early the following morning to go to Belfast. It would take him 4/5 days to organise a meeting of his Committee. He . . . would be prepared to travel North and to recommend the new wording. The AG had told him to expect a communication from the Minister when he arrived home and, if contacted, he could possibly get a "straw" poll on the wording in Belfast the following day. There was a hierarchical structure in his Church which would prevent one person from making a statement. The AG added that all churches felt that they were misquoted last time and therefore any contact with them on this occasion would have to be confidential.

(5) As regards the Methodists, his contact had been the Rev. Desmond Gilliland, Dunkineely, Co. Donegal. Mr. Gilliland was a reasonable man himself but the Methodist Church was the most difficult church from this point of view. The AG had given him the Minister's amendment and his personal response had been favourable. The Southern Committee of the Methodist Church could be assembled fairly quickly. He was expecting a ring from the Minister and the AG suggested that the Minister might meet him over the next few days.

(5) As regards the Society of Friends, the AG suggested that a Mr. David Poole . . . might be contacted.

(7) As regards the Catholic Church, the AG said that he had spoken to the Archbishop of Dublin at some length. The Archbishop had been very conservative

in the course of the discussion and had spoken with some emotion. He had a considerable influence in this matter. He had admitted that there was pressure to have the amendment disposed of without further delay: there was a feeling in Church circles that the protracted debate about the amendment could have serious ill-effects and a perception that a greatly increased number of people were coming likely to vote anti-amendment, because there was no general consensus. On the following day he had rung Monsignor Sheehy. He had put the confirmatory proposal to him. Monsignor Sheehy was conciliatory and did not disagree with the AG's suggestion but said the stage had now been reached when he thought that such a proposal was no longer acceptable. The AG made it clear that the Government had a number of different proposals. Monsignor Sheehy said he was anxious that there should be continuing contact, on the basis of a specific wording rather than generalities, so that action could be taken. Monsignor Sheehy was expecting him to contact him over the weekend but he had deferred doing so until he had spoken to the Minister. The Taoiseach wanted the Protestant churches consulted first as there had been such an effort made to try to meet their point of view to the greatest extent possible.

(8) The draft prepared by Mr. Quigley on 11 March was then discussed. As regards "in particular", the Minister thought this was unacceptable as it would allow further exceptions and defeat the purpose of the amendment. As regards the word "protect" (in the phrase "to protect the life of the mother"), the Protestant churches might accept that only to have it rejected by Monsignor Sheehy. The Minister thought it better to have "save" first. The AG thought that "protect" was better from the drafting point of view and also more effective but agreed that those considerations should not override policy requirements in a negotiating situation. The AG appreciated the reason for suggesting the addition of some such words as "by reason of the fact that it would or might lead to the loss of life of the unborn" but thought this was a drafting matter and could be looked at afterwards. As regards the proposal in the draft for termination of pregnancy in the case of anencephalic pregnancies, the AG said he thought there was no official teaching in the Catholic Church on this. He referred to the view expressed by Mr. Justice Walsh in the *Magee* case that the natural or human rights he had referred to were part of what is generally called the natural law. Judge Walsh regarded the natural law as a theological concept, i.e. the law of God promulgated by reason and the ultimate governor of all the laws of man rather than as an ethical concept and as such a reaffirmation of the ethical content of law in its ideal of justice. However, he added that what exactly natural law is and what precisely it imports is a question which had exercised the minds of theologians for many centuries and on which they were not yet fully agreed. Finally, the AG agreed with the inclusion of "from the commencement of pregnancy" after the Secretary had explained the advantages of doing so, including the fact that it would bring the amendment in this respect into line with the reference in the 1861 Act to "with child". He indicated that he would prefer that the amendment would take the form of an addition to subsection 2° rather than a separate statement.

Note: Later on 14 March the Minister decided that it would be desirable that firm indications should be given to the churches that were being consulted in relation to the important, or "key" words in the revised text. These key expressions were "commencement of *pregnancy*", "shall not be *unlawful*" and "*save* the life".

21 March 1983.

167